Dancing with Wolves
while
Feeding the Sheep

Musings of a Maverick Theologian

Wipf and Stock Publishers
EUGENE, OREGON

Wipf and Stock Publishers
199 West 8th Avenue, Suite 3
Eugene, Oregon 97401

Dancing with Wolves while Feeding the Sheep
Musings of a Maverick Theologian
By Anderson, Ray S.
Copyright©2000 Anderson, Ray S.
ISBN: 1-57910-921-7
Publication date: March, 2002
Previously published by Fuller Seminary Press, 2000.

Table of Contents

Preface	7
1. Introduction: The Making of a Maverick	11
2. Is Jesus an Evangelical?	23
3. Does Jesus Think About Things Today?	35
4. Will Judas be in Heaven?	49
5. What do I Say At the Graveside of a Suicide?	59
6. Did Jesus Have to Die on a Cross?	69
7. Do I Have to Believe in Hell?	79
8. Should I Pray for a Miracle?	89
9. Does God Allow Evil in Order to Produce Good?	101
10 When Does Human Life Begin, and End?	111
11. Musings of a Maverick Theologian	123
References	147

... he broke fresh ground—because, and only because, he had the courage to go ahead without asking whether others were following or even understood. He had no need for the divided responsibility in which others seek to be safe from ridicule, because he had been granted a faith which required no confirmation—a contact with reality, light and intense like the touch of a loved hand; a union in self-surrender without self-destruction, where his heart was lucid and his mind loving. Dag Hammarskjold

Preface

I have not literally danced with wolves. I have fed a flock of sheep, both literally and figuratively, and I am not unacquainted with wolves. During a seven year hiatus from formal educational prior to entering seminary, I operated a farm and ranch for profit, more or less. During that time I acquired a flock of sheep who taught me more by passive resistance than I was later to learn in seminary about congregational leadership. One might say that my continuous role as pastor and teacher of a small church flock while simultaneously mixing it up with faculty seminary colleagues for the past quarter of a century evokes the metaphor of 'dancing with wolves' while feeding the flock! I have adapted my title from the book by Michael Baker, <u>Dances with Wolves.</u> The book was later made into a movie with Kevin Costner playing the role of Lieutenant John Dunbar who was sent to an abandoned army outpost following the Civil War. Dunbar earned the sobriquet from the curious Comanche Indians who observed his nocturnal adventures with a wolf with a regard which bordered on reverence.

There are no mavericks among the sheep. It was from my herd of Hereford cattle raised for beef production that I discovered the maverick syndrome. A new born calf whose mother has died must rustle up its own nourishment by surreptitiously and randomly stealing a supply from nearby unsuspecting cows. These calves are called mavericks. The term itself originated on the cattle range in Texas. Samuel Augustus Maverick (1803-1870) was a prominent Texas pioneer, rancher and statesman, who helped establish the republic of Texas. In 1845 he took a herd of 400 cattle in payment of a debt. He did not brand the cattle. They strayed, and neighboring ranchers called them mavericks. While the name was first given to all unbranded range cattle, it became a term used to describe calves who had lost their mothers. Those calves, in order to survive, had to go from one cow to another in order to steal some milk. As a result, these maverick calves were usually more vigorous than others but were also inherently promiscuous! Only a maverick would dance with the wolves!

A theological maverick is something of this kind. As a faculty member, I earned this label quite honestly, it appears. David Hubbard, the former president of Fuller Theological Seminary, once wrote: "No faculty could handle a whole crew of Ray Andersons. But any faculty would be the poorer without at least one." I took that as a compliment, as any maverick would do!

I have a coffee cup in my office given to me by a student on which is inscribed: "Life can only be understood backwards but it must be lived forwards." The quotation is attributed to the nineteenth century Danish theologian Søren Kierkegaard. I have tried to avoid "living backwards," by living forward, even though it meant opening doors which others had closed and creating windows where others had built walls. If life can only be understood backwards, the time has come for this as well. One must earn the right to muse about life!

I am now completing 41 years of ministry, the first 11 years as full time pastor and 29 years as theological teacher, 25 in the same seminary faculty. I have preached sermons virtually every Sunday for 36 years to only two congregations. Yes, I am feeding the sheep while dancing with wolves!

The chapters which consitute this book are typical of musings—there is no logical order and sequence which connects them. Though I think that the reader will discover some underlying contours of my theological method along with some deeply held convictions. The final chapter includes jottings from my "musing notebook," snapshots from the window of my soul.

Preface

As a no-longer-young maverick, I paraphrase the poignant, and somewhat self indulgent words of the "old soldier," General Douglas McArthur in his farewell speech to Congress, "Old mavericks never die, they just find themselves amusing!"

If you are reading this, it means the corral gate was left open, and one escaped to run again on the open range defying the critic and disturbing the critters who keep to their own close-cropped regimen of rules and results.

1

Introduction: The Making of a Maverick

Lest one think it presumptuous to identify oneself as a maverick, let me respond by saying that only one who truly is a maverick would have the audacity, if not the temerity, to do so. I was a middle child, the second son, with a younger sister. That alone does not qualify. My ancestry included a Norwegian grandmother who left her home and family at the age of 16 to emigrate to the United States, never to return nor ever again to see her own mother and father. She died the year that I was born, so I may have some of her genes but no memory of her face. Her adventuresome spirit, seemingly well domesticated, may have slipped past the unguarded door of her own destiny to beguile an innocent child, a generation removed. It has been known to happen! The maverick spirit, like blue eyes, may be a recessive gene reappearing in the most unlikely disguise of a middle child, bracketed, as it were, by the bookends of predictability and promise.

Her eldest son, my father, was barely 18 when his father died and he quietly assumed the mantle of family provider and shaper of destiny. His birthright was bound to the soil, his spirit harnessed to the routine of planting and reaping, like the animals which bent their will to his bidding. His one attempt to jump the traces and launch a career in business quickly failed and, like a colt with dreams of running with the fast horses in the country fair, he surrendered his vision to a destiny more secure and, as it turned out, at least for him, more sensible.

I early tried to stretch my gait to match his stride, choosing his destiny as my own dream.

As a child, I was not told the story of my grandmother. At that time I assumed that what I had been told was all that was to be told, that what I saw was all there was to see, and that following the footprints of my father would take me to the other side of the narrow sea that was my soul. The inner life of a child is so huge as to be terrifying, and yet so constricted as to be shallow. The spirit of a child is lonesome in its aloneness, echoing the voices which, though silenced by death, still speak in the haunting cry of wild geese flying through a dark spring night. Destiny, mediated through necessity, provides the early contours of a calling which tames the restless spirit and satisfies the hunger of the soul.

There are rituals, sometimes understood only in retrospect, which mark the turning of a page in the story of one's life. Without a hint of self consciousness, and with the skill of a practiced teacher, my father, like Jacob of old, passed on the birthright in the only way that he knew. It happened in this way.

Two sandwiches, a cookie or piece of cake and a small thermos of coffee, twice a day, mid-morning and mid-afternoon. This was my father's lunch when he was working in the field. At the age of 6 or 7, it was usually my task, and not an unhappy one, I am pleased to say, to carry this repast out to him.

These were the days when the farm implements were drawn by horses. While my father quietly ate his lunch, I would pet the horses. On occasion I would slip a stolen sugar cube from my mother's cupboard into the mouth of my favorite, enjoying the slobbering lips against my palm as much as the animal relished the sweet cube. Such were some of my earliest experiences with raw sensuality!

By the time my father had finished the sandwiches and poured his second cup of coffee, I was back at his side, strategically placed for a ritual I had come to expect. Eyeing the piece of cake thoughtfully, he would say, "Well son, I'm not sure I'm up to the cake today, so could you eat it for me while I roll a cigarette?"

While he performed his own ritual of shaking a measured amount of tobacco out of the small cloth sack into the thin paper, licking the edges with his lips and striking a match on the sole of his shoe to light it, I devoured the cake.

The cigarette seemed to lighten the load for him, as well as loosen his tongue. When he talked it was usually as much to himself as it was to me. My role was to listen. It was not, you might say, a real conversation; hardly man to man, and certainly not man to boy! At the same time, in its own way, these times were intensely relational, as I now look back upon them.

He talked about the horses. Each had names so that they could be startled out of their laggard ways by a shout and maybe a touch of the whip when pulling the plow. Like Santa's reindeer, horses respond to their names and their master's voice.

"Star (named for the white splash on his otherwise brown face) is limping a bit, I think we better take a look at his hoof tonight. Might have a stone in it." That was a promise of course, and that evening we, he and I, would examine the foot and perform the simple operation.

The "we" was his language of love. He often used it when speaking of his life and tasks including me as a participant. "We will plant corn in this field next year," he would say, as though I needed to know in order to make my own plans accordingly!

I was not just a boy who carried his lunch, but a partner in the enterprise. He had no need, indeed, no language to talk down to me. Nor did he attempt to treat me as a man with the pretense of "man talk."

What a marvelous word is "we!" While inclusive, it is able to allow for the difference between "you and me" and yet equalizes the disparity of age, gender, race and yes, even religion. What I did when I was alone or with other kids never seemed of much interest to my father. If entering into the games of children and becoming their cheerleader are the skills and duty of parenting, my father was woefully deficient and delinquent. He excelled, however, in the ageless and timeless wisdom of the "we."

As it was, the "me of we" was not big enough for both him and me. My life was narrow and my pursuits were trivial. My peers were competitors as much as they were companions. My siblings were rivals as much as relatives. Yet, his utterance of "we" was as deep as the bond of father and son and as broad as the common destiny on earth that bound man and boy in the struggle between faith and fate.

With utter unselfconsciousness, he drew me out of my own childhood into the "we" of a common life and destiny without destroying the child in me. Perhaps it was out of this unconscious and unspoken wisdom that he was prompted to do something that forever transformed my life.

It happened only once. There was no suggestion that it was planned or premeditated. We were sitting on the edge of the furrow, behind the plow, facing the freshly turned soil over which the seagulls swooped in search of frantic worms. It was the second cup of coffee time. The cigarette lightened the load and loosened his tongue.

"Stick your hand down into the soil, son," he suddenly said without warning. Breaking the rules by looking into my face and talking directly to me. As I did, he said softly, "Son, this soil is part of your life—you take care of it and it will take care of you."

There was, of course, no response expected nor given on my part. I knew the rules and lived by ritual as well. He never spoke of it again, nor did I ever question him about its meaning. It may have been a premonition on his part, of his own transition from a tiller of the soil into the soil itself. Or, it may have simply been the only gift that he knew how to give to me, the wisdom of desire being fulfilled in destiny.

There is a saying that is as old as the hills. "You can take the boy out of the farm but you cannot take the farm out of the boy." I took this as conventional wisdom and as a kind of "manifest destiny" for my life. As if this were not enough, I added to it a paraphrased version that went something like this: "You can take the boy out of or away from the father but you cannot take the father out of the boy."

Following service in the second world war, my sense of attachment to the soil only seemed to grow stronger. While in college, I earned a degree in Agricultural Science and worked part time in the college's farm operations. During my last year, I sold the new car I had purchased with money saved during my military service, and bought a tractor. Arrangements were made to rent a farm back in the community in which I was raised. I did the fall plowing, went back to college and moved, with my family to the farm in the spring.

That spring, as I was in the barn of my rented farm, milking the cows, my parents came to visit. My father sat on a stool watching me for a time. Then quietly said, "Son, it seems that you have finally found what you want in life."

My answer was brief and affirmative. "Yes, dad, this is where I belong." Having retired from his own farm several years earlier due to ill health, it was as though he were now the boy sitting beside the man. He did not say it, but I think he was silently searching for an answer to this question, "Son, are you the we of me?"

Flushed with the excitement of my own venture into life, I do not think I had the wisdom to sense his searching question and say, "This fall, I think **we** will need to remodel this barn to make room for more cows."

That fall, he died quietly of the cancer that ate away at the tissue of his throat and destroyed his voice box so that he could hardly speak. The same cigarettes that lightened his load and loosed his tongue, in the end, had the final say.

For seven years I then pursued my vision and vocation of farming, tracing out my own destiny in the good earth. The legacy of my father became the lengthened shadow of my own place in the sun. To my passion for the soil I added a fascination with the modern technology and the exhilaration of buying and using the latest in farm equipment. I bought and sold, planted and reaped, suffered failures and enjoyed success.

Why was it not enough? Was this not my destiny, to wrestle the soil in submission even while it was working its magic in my heart?

The thought came into my mind like a plant fully grown with no need for soil preparation and planting. I awoke one day and knew that there was something pulling me toward a future that had no antecedent in my past—so I thought! With the revitalizing of personal faith in God that had long lain dormant, I found the words of Jesus Christ to be compelling and unavoidable. In telling the parable of the farmer who kept building bigger barns to store the wealth of his harvests, Jesus said: "But God said to him: 'You fool! This very night your life is being demanded of you. And the things you have prepared, whose will they be?' So it is with those who store up treasures for themselves but are not rich toward God." (Luke 12:20-21).

For more than a year, I struggled with what seemed to be two competing and irresolvable demands upon my life. In general, I had no problem with the idea that one could serve God through farming as well as through any other vocation. But one does not ultimately answer the most fundamental questions about life by theological permission but by existential passion. I knew enough about the Bible to establish theological permission for my calling in life to be a farmer and so fulfill a destiny and live out a gift given to me by my father.

What I didn't find an answer for in the Bible was the lack of inner certainty that this was what would ultimately fulfill my own passion for life. Frankly, I was as much troubled about what I saw as the eventual outcome of my life as a farmer as I was tormented by the question that God had other plans for me! I could fulfill my passion by working the soil, but the soil could not fulfill my passion for a life lived as fully as I knew possible. I had accepted the destiny defined for me by my father, but now I was awakening to a call to leave one land in search of another, in much the same spirit as my grandmother.

God did not call me away from the farm to some form of Christian ministry. I did not leave the farm and attend seminary, preparing for a vocation of pastor and eventually teacher, because I heard a specific call from God. It is seldom as simple as that.

A new and vital life of faith in God, shared with friends and experienced in a community of love and fellowship opened a door which could never again be closed. Through this door my passion spilled out like a river that overruns its banks. At the same time, once this door was open, warm breezes blew in and swept over sleeping segments of my soul. I awakened to what I thought was the sound of God talking, as if to himself, knowing that I was present, "Tomorrow, we will go to those who are like sheep without a shepherd and bring them to a safe place." It was the "we of God" that reached out and included me!

Years later, when I read the words of Christopher Fry, I knew what they meant:

The human heart can go to the lengths of God,
> Dark and cold we may be, but this
> Is no winter now. The frozen misery
> Of centuries breaks, cracks, begins to move;
> The thunder is the thunder of the floes,
> The thaw, the flood, the upstart Spring.
> Thank God our time is now when wrong
> Comes up to face us everywhere,
> Never to leave us till we take
> The longest stride of soul men ever took,
> Affairs are now soulsize.
> The enterprise
> Is exploration into God.

And so **we** left, my family and I, to another state and another life, not daring to look back, not with the fear that one of us would turn into a pillar of salt, but that respect for the dead (though still living) would weaken the resolve to reach the new frontier.

In making the decision to leave the farm and sever the connection that my life had with the soil, I fully expected to suffer, not regret, but a kind of melancholy. It would be, I thought, a kind of death that would leave part of me unattached. In a sense, I felt that I was leaving my father as well as the soil behind.

It was a pleasant shock to discover, even after only a few months, that my new "calling" to study for the Christian ministry had not left an empty space. Nor did I long for what had been or what might have been. What I had thought would be a sacrifice that I would have to make, as the "cross that I had to bear," turned out to be a transplant, roots and all. My career change was not, I think, a kind of denial, but rather a quiet and deeply rooted transplanting of my life from one soil to another.

What my father had long ago discovered, but left for me to find for myself, was that there was neither mystery nor magic in the soil. The mystery and magic, if we dare to use such words, lie in the connection of the heart to the hand. There is no place or task on earth which can satisfy the restless hand which is not attached to the heart.

My father had not attached my hand to the soil on that day long ago, although that was how I had understood it. Rather, he had attached my heart to my hand. My inner self had become bound to my outer life. As a result, whatever task to which I put my hand was done with a sense of finality and completeness that brought joy rather than a feeling of fatalism, which can only produce melancholy and despair. Transplantation without transformation kills the roots as well as the plant. The once in a lifetime gift is one that continues to transform.

How do we account for the shift of passion from one objective to another? How do we explain the inner certainty with which we change direction without doubting the correctness of the first and without questioning the rightness of the next?

Did I unknowingly stumble into some kind of "transforming power" through which I reached for more than the soil could offer? It is surely a paradox. My father taught me that my integrity could be measured by how I planted a straight row of corn. This is the same man who also empowered me to reach out for a personal goal and life fulfillment beyond the world that ended with the last row of corn!

I did not leave my father sitting on a stool waiting for me to give him a life. Nor did I betray him by pulling my plow out of the ground for the last time, and leave without his permission. At one time, part of me thought that way, but no more.

The "we of God" has room in it for both my father and me. When God whispered, "Tomorrow we will go to those who are like sheep without a shepherd," I became a partner of God. The "we of God" equalizes our relation without confusing or distorting the difference between us. God does not talk down to me, as a man to a child, nor does he attempt to treat me as divine with the pretense of "God talk."

Following a decade of ministry as a pastor of a church which emerged from an orange grove to a vibrant congregation, my spirit stirred within me to reach out for yet another venture. Two years of study at the University of Edinburgh in Scotland, leading to a doctoral degree in theology, resulted in a teaching career now spanning 30 years.

I did not intend to be a scholar and was faithful to that intention, except for the books written to avoid the fate of an unproductive seminary professor, "publish or parish!" The 7 year hiatus in my formal education prior to entering seminary was followed by another 11 year interim during which I served as pastor of a church prior to entering doctoral studies which eventually led to my present teaching position at a theological seminary. At the outset of my professorial career I was soon to discover that being a teacher was quite different than being a scholar, though I was hired for the former and paid for the latter! The discipline of scholarship, which I had already discovered during my Ph.D. studies, involved research and writing by which one's intellectual mettle was demonstrated in copious, critical and continuous footnotes. In these notes, dialogue with other scholars was sustained as a kind of running commentary beneath or alongside of one's own contribution. When one's own writing and thinking became the subject of critical note and interaction by other writers, then one was thought to be a scholar.

For the reader, however, footnotes can often be a distraction if not a diversion. For example, a passing comment offered during a round table discussion as to what scholarly style we should use in a forthcoming publication resulted in this conversation stopper: "Coming across a footnote in reading a text is somewhat like having the doorbell ring when making love to one's wife!"

Never mind that the Apostle Paul managed to get his letters published without footnotes and, as some have lamented, without much editorial supervision! Never mind that one could transform a five acre orange grove and a dozen families into a flourishing congregation over an 11 year period with well established footing but no footnotes!

The playing field was not level, as I soon discovered; my (metaphorical) mother had disappeared and I was left to run the range by myself, relying upon my instincts and intuition. Along the way I wore the prescribed uniform, punctuated my writings with footnotes, while nourishing my maverick tendencies into a rather full grown, aging, but agile creature of a special kind.

Lewis Smedes, my former colleague once told me that nearing retirement he told the President of our seminary, "I have written my last book with footnotes!" Fortunately for him (my fortune is more penurious), his literary craft, inspired prose, and unerring instinct for the deeper yearnings of the human spirit resulted in several best-sellers. Theological mavericks may sometimes transgress boundaries, but they do not lack passion. They may fall short of conformity but not curiosity. They may often tease, and sometimes tread on toes, but always with a twinkle in their eyes.

To write without copious footnotes as a mark of scholarship is an audacious undertaking, even for a maverick. At the same time, I take no credit for originality when I come upon something I wish I had thought of, but didn't. Rather than using footnotes to document such sources, I have placed all references at the end of the book.

What follows are musings, such as one might find in the company of busy pastors and "laid back" seminary profs who, free from the restraints of polished sermons and prepared lectures, reflect out loud on the issues which both torment and tantalize the practitioner and bearer of Word of God. I have come to see that theology must be more than merely making Word of God relevant to modern culture, for what is relevant today is irrelevant tomorrow. Theology must be more than merely being contemporary, for what is contemporary in one day is already obsolete for another. Theology must be more than useful, for what is useful to one person may also be harmful to another. Theology, rather, is servant to Word of God. The mandate laid upon theology is that it be effective Word of God, as God himself said through the prophet, "so shall my word be that goes out from my mouth; it shall not return to me empty, but it shall accomplish that which I purpose, and succeed in the thing for which I sent it" (Isaiah 55:11). I lean toward the purpose of God expressed through the Word and Work of God. "Tell the truth, but tell it slant—" wrote Emily Dickinson. Theology, from a Maverick's perspective, is putting a slant on Word of God.

Two young women were overhead in the halls of a college classroom building discussing their personal life, centering around one of the woman's recent breakup with her boyfriend. She was ranting and raving about the way in which she was treated until the other finally said, "I will tell you what I would do. I would just take a philosophical approach to the whole thing."

"So what does that mean?"

"Just try not to think about it."

I am not a philosopher, but I do try to think about things. My musings are not meant to be rantings nor ravings, but probing and productive exercises in creative theological thinking. These pieces are not meant to offer conclusive answers to the questions raised, but to stimulate more thought. My hope is that the reader will indeed want to continue to think further about it after completing each chapter.

Not as earthy as Luther's "Table Talk," nor as clever as C. S. Lewis's "Screwtape Letters," my style is that of a theological maverick—I rove about promiscuously but sleep in one fold with those who call themselves 'evangelicals.'

Now I muse on this question, "Is Jesus an Evangelical?"

2

Is Jesus an Evangelical?

The question came through under the radar, from the side, but with the impact of a full frontal strike. The context was more of a conversation than a confrontation. It came from a young man, speaking for a new generation of African American Christians who want to take what Jesus said about justice and righteousness seriously, as though it had to do with making things right rather than merely right thinking. "You evangelicals never want to get caught out in public without your label attached. Was Jesus an evangelical?"

In reflecting on the anecdote, what strikes me is not so much the sharp point of the question as the broad brush stroke of the label—"you evangelicals." I had become quite comfortable with the expression, "we evangelicals" believe such and such; "we evangelicals" have this in common; "we evangelicals" know that Jesus was divine and the Bible infallible. It didn't really strike me until the question hit its mark, how easy it is for 'we' to become 'them.' When our belief becomes canned with a semantic label it can easily become a liability by being put on a shelf.

"You evangelicals"—Am I one of 'them?' I must confess that I am, by birth as well as choice. Baptized and confirmed in the Evangelical Lutheran Church in the upper Midwest, I was labeled early and often. Discovering that the Evangelical Lutheran Church was known as the 'Norwegian Synod,' I came to see that it was not sufficient for these folk to distinguish themselves from the Swedish and German Lutherans in that rural village by nationality, so they had to add the word 'Evangelical' in order to clinch their hold on the truth. No matter that in the European post-reformation ecclesial community, to say that one was both Lutheran and Evangelical was at best a redundancy.

My ordination into pastoral ministry was in the Evangelical Free Church, where I served as Pastor for eleven years and still hold credentials in that denomination. Here too I discovered that it was not enough to be an Evangelical Lutheran, for spiritual nominalism and State control of the church led to the formation of a movement that was both Evangelical and Free! I have published a chapter on "Evangelical Theologians" (<u>The Modern Theologians</u>, Blackwell, 1997), and have now served a quarter of a century on the faculty of a theological seminary that defines itself as having evangelical commitment as well as 'evangelical fervor.' I live in the shadow of the 'giants' of evangelical theology and mission. These are the 20th century scholars, leaders, and evangelists who coined the phrase 'new evangelical' and founded both a national evangelical journal as well as seminaries and colleges.

I suspect that calling myself an 'evangelical Christian' is an attempt to position myself alongside of Jesus as much as it is to partition myself off from others. If so, then I wonder whether the label has not become a liability, if not also libelous. When some Christians at Corinth claimed Jesus as a partisan to gain sectarian advantage on the playing field of personal piety, the apostle Paul delivered a well deserved rebuke. He was appalled to hear that some were using labels in their claim for spiritual orthodoxy. It was bad enough that some were claiming to "belong to Peter," and others to "belong to Paul," but when some sought to put the rest down by claiming to "belong to Christ," contentious piety had become pretentious arrogance (1 Cor. 1:11-12). Lord help us!

When it comes to piety, it is hard to be both right and righteous. When it is a matter of theology, those who call themselves evangelical, like all who take their stand on being right, are finding that it is difficult to be correct while remaining humble. Arrogance may not be among the seven deadly sins, but it is in the top ten.

The root of arrogance lies deeply imbedded in human nature fallen away from the grace of God. Adam and Eve succumbed to the temptation to be "like God" in taking of the forbidden fruit (Gen. 3:5). This is the root arrogance. The fruit of arrogance is produced from the branches of division, distrust and finally destruction of human life. Though religion is not the root of arrogance, it becomes fertile soil for its growth. As Karl Barth once said, "The call to worship can be the temptation to idolatry," even though this is a "call which cannot be avoided." I would paraphrase Barth by saying, "The call to follow Jesus can lead to the slippery slope of arrogance." To label oneself as holding some special truth about God is already to sip the sweet nectar of arrogance.

When claims to religious truth are used to deflect criticism, deliver ultimatums, and destroy opponents, arrogance has raised its ugly head regardless of the brand name. Arrogance can flourish in the religious mind and Christianity is no exception. Fundamentalism and liberalism alike can become its breeding ground. Evangelicalism as a reaction to both fundamentalism and liberalism is not immune. Too often, evangelicals have often sought to gain a sense of identity by setting themselves apart from fundamentalism and liberalism, rather than humbly admitting roots in one and a certain coziness with the other.

Resorting to labels is often libelous when used to maintain a space on the top of the mountain by crowding others off, especially when it is mount Zion. Calling oneself an 'evangelical,' if the label is meant as certification of theological correctness and personal piety, implies that those who do not proudly wear the label are somehow inferior, if not heretical. The odor of arrogance can be difficult to detect by those who confuse it with a fragrant offering, well pleasing to the Lord! Those who do not merit the label 'evangelical' can usually sniff out the aroma of arrogance from quite a distance.

Can we who wear the label 'evangelical' enjoy the sweet fragrance of fellowship with our spiritual kinfolk without exuding the odor of arrogance? Can we seek to embody the character of Christ without making it a form of "character armor" worn with moral smugness? Can we seek to become the community of Christ without claiming ecclesial purity by excluding others? Can we uphold orthodox doctrines about Christ without claiming doctrinal hegemony? These are questions I ask of myself and invite others to ask with me.

My purpose here is to see what arrogance might look like when it takes a particular evangelical form. My thesis is that the person of Jesus Christ is the antidote to the root of arrogance as a fundamental flaw in human nature. Jesus destroyed the root of arrogance in humanity by humbly living in conformity with God's divine purpose. Through his unique relation with God as the Son of the Father empowered and directed by the Spirit, Jesus prepared in his own humanity the form of true humanity as bearing God's image. Only when we view our own spiritual identity through the prism of Jesus' character, can we detect the arrogance lurking in the deepest recesses of our evangelical piety as well as our orthodox theological pronouncements.

When I warn of evangelical arrogance, I do so as one who is more than likely prone to the temptation. As a reminder to myself and, I hope, a disarming word to those who feel themselves fortunate not to wear this label, these words are written.

The Arrogance of Moral Smugness

The posture of *moral smugness* on the part of some evangelicals is often perceived as arrogance. I think of the phrase, "I love the sinner but hate the sin." When this is said with a smile, if not a smirk, it comes across as arrogant. While it is a benign kind of arrogance it often displays an exhilarating lack of self doubt!

To claim the virtue of love in order to make one immune from the criticism of being judgmental while labeling the behavior of others as sin is a form of moral self indulgence.

One cannot claim love as a moral virtue while holding the object of love at a distance. How does this help the recipient of such a platitude? I suspect that the underlying motive for saying this to anyone is basically self serving.

For example, some label homosexuality sinful and a perversion while, at the same time claim the higher moral ground of love for the sinner. It is not the distinction between moral and immoral behavior that leads to arrogance; we expect such moral discernment of all persons who possess moral character. To assume a moral prerogative to judge another person's sin by claiming the moral virtue of love can have the appearance of arrogance and smacks of moral smugness. Being right without being loving causes us to see only the sin and not the sinner at all. Jesus' harshest words were directed toward the sin of arrogance clothed in self righteousness. For those caught in moral contradictions and spiritual contrariness, he expressed compassion and opened up access to divine love and empowering grace as a means healing and hope.

A lack of a sense of the tragic in dealing with moral complexity as a human condition begets moral smugness. To be pro-life in principle and hold that the death of a fetus at any stage of development is a tragic loss points to a violation of the moral good which we attribute to life as both potential and actual. One can hold this as a moral principle without moral smugness as long as it does not become a claim to moral virtue by labeling all who disagree as "baby killers." The moral context of life is often layered and complex, with 'good' competing with 'good,' not simply good versus evil. This is the essence of the tragic. Failure to recognize this can lead to the arrogant assertion of one's own 'good,' as a moral right even if it means violence against the rights, if not the persons, of others.

One could wish that good and evil could always be separated with surgical precision, and that moral virtue could be achieved by making moral judgments. Alas, it is not so. We who make moral judgments suffer ourselves from moral ambiguity if not also moral fault. In an effort to earn the right to wear the label 'evangelical,' I fear that many seek out issues on which to make absolute moral pronouncements. Responsible moral discernment and action bears a sense of the tragic, as Dietrich Bonhoeffer demonstrated. Where good and evil are inextricably bound up in the fabric of our own existence, responsibility to act on behalf of the victim of injustice, oppression and abuse is a moral responsibility. But in such actions we may not be able to claim moral innocence as measured by abstract moral principles. As Bonhoeffer pointed out, Jesus himself entered into the realm of moral ambiguity and finally bore the legal penalty of moral guilt in order to redeem those without moral standing. If this is what we mean by evangelical witness to the truth, it is less likely to leave behind the odor of arrogance nor reek of moral smugness.

The Arrogance of Ecclesial Purity

Another facet of evangelical arrogance is reflected in an attempt to attain *ecclesial purity* when it comes to drawing the boundary between the church and the world or, as is often the case, between "my church and your church." I have already mentioned as part of my own evangelical credentials, ordination with the Evangelical Free Church of America, a denomination of modest size which emerged among the nineteenth century immigrants from Scandinavia. Seeking to escape what was perceived as nominalism and outright unbelief among the Lutheran State churches, their concern for authentic Christian faith and personal relationship with the Lord led to the formation of congregations whose members were "believer's only," the title of a book published by a former President of the Evangelical Free Church. Their impulse for ecclesial purity can be understood in the context of their concern for authentic Christian life and faith.

Being himself something of a tragic figure, the Danish theologian, Søren Kierkegaard, applied the rapier edge of his own rhetoric to a similar situation when he wrote, "if everyone is a Christian no one is." Whatever the evangelical passion by which he scorned and scolded the established church, Kierkegaard could hardly be charged with being arrogant.

Defining faith in such radical terms that he confessed himself not to have attained, he pointed to evangelical existence rather than to an evangelical church. Among the early immigrants who carved out their own existence in the untamed and sometimes treacherous frontiers of the new world, I sensed something of the same concern. It was the authenticity of evangelical existence rather than the creating of an evangelical church that directed their passion and inspired their mission. Unfortunately, it was not long before the issue of purity became a synonym for piety.

It is hard to be both right and righteous. When the evangelical church sets itself apart from the world for the sake of its own purity rather than manifest authentic Christian existence in the world, arrogance is inevitable. In a book that has received less recognition than it deserves, Hans Küng suggested that the church should never claim to be the true church, but instead, be a truthful church. Does the church help people become truthfully Christian—to be truthfully human, asked Küng? A truthful church, he argued, is one that is provisional, that is, is not an end in itself; it is unassuming, that is, not be constantly in need of grace but rather in dispensing it; it is ministering, that is, to take the way of the cross rather than the way of triumphal procession. A truthful church is conscious of guilt, that is, to remain free from all claims except the radical will of God as revealed in Jesus Christ.

The quest for ecclesial purity as a mark of an evangelical church is a protestant version of Küng's critique. Forced to define evangelical existence by how one looks and behaves in being different from the world rather than one's conformity to Christ who exists in the world, results in legalism and separatism. Those who rather smugly insisted that they were truly Christian because they did not reek of tobacco began to stink of a different odor—that of arrogance. Across the board, regardless of ethnic origin or denominational tradition, in the melting pot of North American ecclesial culture, evangelicalism has become as much a defining label as a transforming life experience. When the word "evangelical" becomes a label it can easily become a liability. When the word is used to define what is exclusive, like flowers pulled from their stems and roots, the odor at first is sweet and pungent, but soon becomes cloying and offensive—as does the odor of arrogance.

The Arrogance of Doctrinal Hegemony

Coupled with the concern for ecclesial purity, like the ribs and rods that support a tent, is the tendency toward *doctrinal hegemony* or, to put it more simply, an exclusive claim for doctrinal truth. The quest for an exclusive doctrinal truth represents, in part, the rationalism of a post-enlightenment, modern view of reality. The thrust of Jesus' self testimony was "I am the way, the truth and the life." When this takes the form of a propositional truth it is expressed more abstractly as "he is the truth." The shift from Christ to Christology and from confession to creed marked the early church's struggle against heresy. As long as the creeds were "sung" as part of the liturgy of a believing and worshipping community, the doctrine of Christ was the theological handmaid to devotion to Christ.

Following the enlightenment, the quest for universal truth as expressed in propositional form took precedence over revelational truth. Theological orthodoxy became a matter of definition rather than devotion. The modern mindset was critical of claims for truth based on historical evidences and personal experience. Theological orthodoxy sought refuge in propositional truth which became the objective basis for evangelical piety. Like the leaning tower of Pisa, however, orthodoxy soon discovered that a foundational theology based on critical modern rationalism lost its grip on revealed truth and began to tilt. In sowing the wind of modernity, to use a biblical metaphor, the orthodoxy reaped the whirlwind of modernism (Hosea 8:7). Out of this was born the modern evangelical movement.

The emergence of the movement called fundamentalism in the early part of the 20th century has been well documented and closely analyzed. For the most part, the first wave were preachers and evangelists scandalized by the tidal wave of modernism sweeping across the revered centers of theological study and seeping into the strategic nerve centers of mainline Protestant denominational leadership. Not only did they fear the loss of biblical authority under the scalpel of liberal biblical criticism, but also the loss of evangelistic zeal and mission imperative resulting from capitulation to modern cultural pluralism. When they identified the problem as erosion of theological truth and departure from orthodox doctrine, they redefined the faith in terms of certain 'fundamentals' to which one had to subscribe in order to be 'evangelical.'

I do not detect the odor of arrogance among these early fundamentalists. They were street fighters, as it were! One might say that they lacked the sophistication to be arrogant! Their descendents, however, who earned doctoral degrees from prestigious university divinity schools, were not satisfied with being in the truth, but took it upon themselves to explain why they and no one else held the truth. Doctrinal hegemony is a more sophisticated form of fundamentalism, but possesses the same instincts—to defend truth by doctrinal definition. Using these definitions to stake an exclusive claim on truth is doctrinal hegemony and tends to have the odor of arrogance.

Evangelicalism was conceived in the marriage of experiential piety and theological orthodoxy. Each by itself is tolerable. But somehow in the mix of being right and being righteous there exudes toxic vapors which, without the fresh breath of the Holy Spirit, can smolder into the fumes of arrogance.

Arrogance is difficult to maintain without shooting one's own wounded.

Edward John Carnell, one of my former professors, who himself made the journey from fundamentalism to evangelicalism, called fundamentalism, "Orthodoxy gone cultic." He sought to retain the doctrinal formulations of a pre-fundamentalist orthodoxy but with the addition of the law of love as an epistemological as well as a moral imperative. He was bitterly attacked by his former fundamentalist friends but also by some of his new-evangelical colleagues for placing love alongside of truth as a criterion for orthodoxy. Unable to sustain his physical and emotional health, he was left behind, weary and wounded, in the "battle for the Bible." His premature death ended the paradox of his life in true Kierkegaardian style. Tragic, is the epitaph many would write over the legacy of this man. Tortured and truthful, is my own estimation. For all of his commitment to orthodox theology, he wore the label 'evangelical' with uneasy self consciousness. I think that he truly feared arrogance in himself as well as in his early apologetics for the faith.

Labels can be libelous, as I have said. Am I guilty? Perhaps. But to call myself an evangelical is not only a label, it can also be a liability for what, otherwise, should be considered a worthy endeavor—to speak the truth in love. Moral smugness, ecclesial purity, and doctrinal hegemony are liabilities for which there is no license in representing the gospel of Jesus Christ in the world.

Was Jesus an evangelical? No, he was the *evangel*, in his person and in his actions, the embodiment of both grace and truth (John 1:17). His moral presence was both convicting and empowering. He drew to his side the fugitive from the law as well as the furtive Pharisee, without shaming either.

He ignored the categories established within his own society. For him the despised Samaritan was a woman who could give <u>him</u> a drink, the self righteous Pharisee a man who wanted to talk, the leper a person who needed to be touched. While people came to him in crowds, needs came with a name. A congregation was not a mob to be sent home to eat, but individuals to be fed with bread broken with his own hands. In a crowd he was never simply pushed by people, but touched by someone who was hurting. Within the shouting sounds of a multitude he heard the cry of the blind man, the sigh of a sinner, the murmur of a skeptic. He let people be the way they were and offered to help them become who they could be. He had no uniforms for his disciples and no masks for his friends. He did not ask for conformity but for the commitment of love. His style was love, his pattern devotion.

In the person of Jesus there was a spiritual integrity that revitalized the spirit of human persons amidst the dead weight of tradition and legalism—where Jesus was there was life. In the life of Jesus was a moral integrity that brought an absolute sense of righteousness to specific human situations—where Jesus was there was truth. In the truth of Jesus there was a personal integrity that spoke with authority against the enslaving influences of religious formalism and demonic delusion—where Jesus was there was freedom.

In the midst of a religious culture that prized appearance and cultivated form, he appeared among us clothed simply in grace and truth. He refused to recognize as spiritual that which was artificial and affected. He valued the truth of being and doing over the self righteousness of words and prayers. He told it like it was—both in the street and in the temple. He had one language for both the saint and the sinner. He stated divine realities in terms of human experience. His life-style was that of a human person living among humans. Because he <u>was</u> the truth, he had no fear of exposure, nothing to defend. Because he was <u>human,</u> he had no fear of humanness, in himself or others.

Because he understood and accepted his own humanity, he never condemned another for being human. He demonstrated that a holy purpose can only be completed when the spirit and the flesh become one. He was in every sense a mature person: his feelings ran deep but they had a foundation; his love flowed freely and yet within boundaries; he was sensitive to pain but not easily hurt; he had a dream, but consecrated his life in duty.

He came as a Son and introduced God as the Father. Out of this relationship he gave new meaning to words which captured human problems and possibilities: prodigal, enemy, reconciliation, friend, brother and sister, flock. He defined spiritual values in terms of human relationships. God forgives us as we forgive one another; to hate our brother is to hate God; to give of ourselves to another is to love Christ. He gave himself as the new basis for the community of persons. Those who love Christ become his body, with a common life and one heart.

He liberated the spirit from the law and created children of God from persons in all forms of slavery. He lifted the burden of the law by fulfilling it, not by breaking it, and pointed beyond it to a higher fulfillment. Those who become slaves in his kingdom find their freedom. In his own life, he brought both body and soul into balance.

He brought a new degree of tolerance to the sharp edge of divine justice. He held back the law long enough for people to discover <u>why</u> they were law breakers, and to receive mercy. He brought a new spirit of liberality into the up-tightness of a religiously structured society. He taught that the sabbath was made for humans, not humans for the sabbath; everything doesn't have to be perfect to please God, and pleasing God is more important than pleasing others. He brought a new dimension of practicality to the word love. Love from God can be worn on the back, put on the table and sit down beside you—it is human as well as divine, tangible as well as spiritual. It is Jesus.

As an antidote to arrogance, as Scripture reminds us, we ought not to look at our own "natural face" in a mirror, but to view our spiritual identity through the prism of Jesus' person and character (James 1:23-24). Only then will we detect the arrogance lurking in the deepest recesses of our evangelical piety as well as our orthodox theological pronouncements. The question is not, did Jesus look like an evangelical? The question is, are evangelicals willing to look like Jesus! Think about it!

3

Does Jesus Think About Things Today?

"Can I assume that all of you would give assent to the statement that the resurrection of Jesus from the dead included his body and not just his spirit?" The classroom of pastors enrolled in our Doctor of Ministry program all nodded in agreement. Some, anxious to reinforce their evangelical credentials even raised their hand, thinking that we were voting on the issue. "How many of you," I then asked, "have considered that if Jesus was raised bodily from the grave that his brain was reconstituted as well so that he could have new ideas, thoughts, and intentions? In other words, does Jesus think about things today?"

"I hadn't thought about that," one pastor said. "Then think about it," I responded. "If the body of Jesus was raised, and his brain also, then do you think that Jesus has ever had a new idea or thought concerning God's purpose for the past two millennia? If so, how do you think that he would communicated that to us?"

There was a moment of stunned silence. "Or," I suggested, "Do you think that he is just sitting at the right hand of the Father leaving us with the Bible and the words he spoke to us before he ascended to heaven without having anything new to say?"

The discussion which ensued revealed a great deal of concern as to what this would mean with regard to the Bible as our sole source of revelation. Some protested that it would be very dangerous to think that "new revelation" could occur after the closing of the biblical canon as a final authority. "Sola Scriptura," one pastor suggested was the formula under-girding Luther's stance against the claims of the medieval church for an authority alongside of or beyond the Bible.

"What then is the role of the Holy Spirit as the continuing witness to the presence of Jesus in our midst?" The responses generally went in two directions. Those who considered themselves in the Reformed theological tradition, argued that the Holy Spirit's role was to "illuminate" the text of Scripture, guiding the reader into the true intent and purpose of Word of God. Others, more in line with the Pentecostal tradition, suggested that the Holy Spirit's role was that of a personal filling or "baptism" of the Spirit resulting in the charismata, or gifts of the Spirit, enriching the devotional life and empowering the ministry of the church. When pressed, those in the pentecostal tradition admitted that even such phenomena of the Spirit's presence and work must be strictly in line with biblical teaching.

As it turned out, both those in the Reformed and Pentecostal theological tradition were unwilling to allow for the contemporary presence and work of Jesus through the Spirit as a narrative text of God's work to be placed alongside of the narrative text of God's Word (the Bible). When I asserted that the Work of God is the hermeneutical criterion for Word of God, red flags went up all over the room! This was their first encounter with a maverick theologian!

In this chapter I want to draw out the implications of my assertion. If we consider the Scriptures of both the Old and New Testament to be narratives of God's self revelation through word and deed, as experienced by and recorded by those who had the original encounter, then the text of Scripture may be considered to be a narrative text transmitted first by oral tradition and then by Spirit inspired written form. This narrative text is what we have come to call "Word of God," Holy Scripture, the Bible.

Within this narrative text, however, there is evidence of

another text at work which constituted an interpretive or hermeneutical criterion. For example, the narrative text of the Law of Moses had become the authoritative Word of God concerning the keeping of the sabbath. Jesus, as the contemporary, incarnate, Word of God (John 1:14) experienced the Work of God in his life and ministry in such a way that another "narrative text" emerged. The healing of the man on the sabbath, who was born blind, constituted just such a "text" of God's work which revealed a deeper truth concerning the sabbath than the narrative text of the law was understood to contain. Faced with the fact that the man had been healed (which by now has become a narrative text), those who opposed Jesus reviled the man, saying, "You are his disciple, but we are disciples of Moses" (John 9:28). Jesus did not claim to break or destroy the law of Moses, but to fulfill it in accordance with God's purpose for the restoration of broken and estranged humanity (Matt. 5:17; Luke 24:44). Contrary to his contemporary's understanding of the sabbath, Jesus interpreted the law of the sabbath in accordance with God's work on the sabbath to mean that "The sabbath was made for humankind, and not humankind for the sabbath" (Mark 2:27).

The saying of Jesus thus became a new text of Word of God, but only as a result of the narrative text of the Work of God.

When we look at the ministry and teaching of the Apostle Paul we can find the same correlation of the two kinds of narrative texts. Paul was well aware that circumcision was a commandment of God given to Abraham and reiterated by Moses to the effect that no uncircumcised Gentile should be counted as righteous before God in the same way as a Jew. Following Paul's dramatic conversion on the Damascus road where he met the resurrected and ascended Jesus and was "filled with the Holy Spirit" (Acts 9:17), he encountered the work of the risen Christ in the coming of the Spirit upon Gentiles.

The narrative text of Peter's encounter with the Holy Spirit in speaking of Jesus to the household of Cornelius, a Gentile, and the immediate Baptism of the uncircumcised Cornelius and his household into Christ would have been well known to Paul after his conversion (Acts 10). Thus, when Paul encountered the same phenomenon in his ministry to the Gentiles, he concluded that circumcision had come to an end in Christ as had all of the law of Moses (Romans 10:4).

When he was called to defend his position before the heads of the church in Jerusalem, he argued that his "text" was actually the lives of the Gentile Christians who had been filled with the Spirit of Christ. To the Corinthians Paul wrote: "Have I not seen Jesus our Lord? Are you not my work in the Lord?... for you are the seal of my apostleship in the Lord" (1 Cor. 9:1-2). In the face of the leaders of the church in Jerusalem who were using the "text of Moses" in demanding circumcision of the Gentiles, and thus upsetting the faith of the Christians at Corinth, Paul wrote: "You yourselves are our letter, written on our hearts, to be known and read by all; and you show that you are a letter of Christ, prepared by us, written not with ink but with the Spirit of the living God, not on tablets of stone but on tablets of human hearts" (2 Corinthians 3:2,3). This is what I mean by a narrative text of the work of God which serves as a hermeneutical criterion for the Word of God. Again, we must agree that the result was a new narrative text of Scripture so that Paul's letters were recognized as "Scripture" in the same sense as the Old Testament. This fact Peter himself later came to see when he wrote that Paul's letters, though containing some things hard to understand, must be considered along with the "other scriptures" (2 Peter 3:16).

So far I have attempted to show that the Work of God can be understood not only as the source of Word of God, but that the Work of God, as in the Work of Christ as the power and presence of the Holy Spirit, must also be a narrative text along side of the existing narrative text of Scripture. The fact that Scripture itself forces us to this conclusion can be demonstrated as I have attempted to do above.

In agreeing to this one has not yet been confronted with

the force of my thesis that the risen and ascended Christ is our contemporary in the form of the present work of the Holy Spirit in such a way that where the Spirit is, there is the Lord. "Now the Lord is the Spirit, and where the Spirit of the Lord is, there is freedom" (2 Cor. 3:17).

In following my argument, several assumptions must be understood. First, the work of God through Christ became a narrative text which served as a critical criterion for interpreting and applying the narrative Scripture text. Second, Christ's work as the work of God took place through the power of the Spirit of God. "But if it is by the Spirit of God that I cast out demons, then the kingdom of God has come to you" (Matthew 12:28). Third, following the resurrection Jesus breathed the Spirit upon his disciples with the promise that through the Spirit his own authority to minister the Work of God on earth would continue (John 20:22).

Fourth, the presence and power of the Holy Spirit following Pentecost was assumed by the first century church to be equal to the words of Jesus prior to his crucifixion. Thus, Paul virtually equates the words of the historical Jesus carried forward by his disciples with Paul's own teaching as having the "mind of Christ" (1 Cor. 2:16). This led to the practical application that Paul's teaching contained both. For example, "To the married I give this command—not I but the Lord—..." (1 Cor. 7:10). "To the rest I say—I and not the Lord—..." (1 Cor. 7:12). "Now concerning virgins, I have no command of the Lord, but I give my opinion as one who by the Lord's mercy is trustworthy" (1 Cor. 7:25). Paul's confidence in placing his own teaching alongside that of the historical Jesus is that the same Jesus is now guiding him through the Spirit.

Finally, I assume that the Holy Spirit is not only the Spirit of the historical Jesus as a contemporary Christ but is the Spirit of the coming, eschatological, Christ. Thus the Holy Spirit makes contemporary the Christ who is to come and who will give the final verdict as to what constitutes the will of Christ through the life and ministry of the Church as the body of Christ. Paul is quite clear about this regarding his own teaching and ministry.

"Think of us in this way, as servants of Christ and stewards of God's mysteries. Moreover, it is required of stewards that they be found trustworthy. But with me it is a very small thing that I should be judged by you or by any human court. I do not even judge myself. I am not aware of anything against myself, but I am not thereby acquitted. It is the Lord who judges me. Therefore do not pronounce judgment before the time, before the Lord comes, who will bring to light the things now hidden in darkness and will disclose the purposes of the heart. Then each one will receive commendation from God" (1 Corinthians 4:1-5).

From this I assume that the resurrected and coming Christ enters now into the present time as our contemporary, creating new narratives of Christ's work by the Spirit through which we are to read and interpret the textual narrative of Holy Scripture. These contemporary narratives of the work of the Spirit do not become Holy Scripture, nor revelation in the same way that Scripture itself is. However, the contemporary narratives as evidence of the work of Christ serve as hermeneutical criteria in reading and applying the Scripture narratives as Word of Christ.

Let me provide some examples.

My preparation for ministry took place between 1956 and 1959 in a seminary consisting of approximately 300 students of which 292 were male and 8 were female. The female students were not allowed to earn the B.D. degree but had to enroll in the M.R.E. degree (Master of Religious Education). They were not permitted to take courses in biblical languages nor in exegetical study of Scripture with the assumption that they could not be ordained and serve as pastors, but only as teachers and educators. My recollection is that the female students did not complain but had come with the understanding that the seminary faculty were convinced that Scripture did not permit the ordination of women for pastoral ministry.

In the 1960s, something happened. A larger number of

female students came to the seminary with the expectation that they should be allowed to take courses leading to ordination in their respective churches. Their argument was not based on ideological feminism nor on the cultural changes regarding the role of women in society. Rather, they simply said that their churches had affirmed their calling and anointing by the Holy Spirit for pastoral ministry and had sent them to be prepared for ordination to this ministry.

The faculty were in somewhat of a quandary. Their first response was to create a new degree especially for the female students enabling them to take courses in biblical exegesis, but to retain the B. D. degree exclusively for men. The absurdity of this soon became apparent, and certain of the faculty took seriously the fact that the churches which were sending these women to be prepared for ordination may not all be disobedient to Scripture. As a result, when the theologians went back to read the text of Scripture from this perspective, they exclaimed in effect, "What do you know! We now see ways in which we can exegete the text so as to allow women to be prepared for ordination in the church."

In retrospect, I have concluded that if the number of female students had not increased and had not challenged the faculty with regard to the role of the church in affirming these women as led by the Spirit, the seminary to this day would still hold that only males should be given pastoral leadership in the church, a view which many seminaries still hold.

I have two comments regarding this narrative. First, the response of the theologians on the faculty was to find a new exegetical basis for the their decision to allow female students to receive the B. D. degree in preparation for ordination. This resulted in some tortured exegetical maneuvers which, at least in the case of one of my former teachers and later a colleague on the faculty, led to the conclusion that the Apostle Paul was simply wrong in what he wrote to Timothy forbidding women to teach and have authority over men in the church. After publishing his conclusions he was censored by the Trustees but allowed to continue teaching. And, more importantly, the faculty continued to accept women into the B. D. degree program based, at least in part, on his position.

My second comment on this case is that the faculty basically failed to grasp the hermeneutical implications of the "narrative text" provided by the women who came under the authority and sponsorship of their churches. Instead of viewing the work of the Holy Spirit in anointing these women for ministry as Pastors as a text to be read alongside of their reading of the biblical text, the faculty turned back toward new and creative exegetical devices in order to find in Scripture the basis for what was, in fact, a rather pragmatic solution to their dilemma, even at the risk of playing one Scripture text against another.

My point is this. Confronted with the narrative text represented by the presence and testimony of these women students backed up by the discernment of the church that the Spirit of Christ indeed was at work, the hermeneutical significance of this narrative text was ignored. I have argued elsewhere that the resurrection of Christ as a contemporary reality of the Spirit constitutes a hermeneutical criterion equivalent to that recognized by Peter when he gave his narrative account of the baptism of Cornelius. After recounting the incident before the leaders of the church at Jerusalem, Peter said, "And as I began to speak, the Holy Spirit fell upon them just as it had upon us at the beginning... If then God gave them the same gift that he gave us when we believed in the Lord Jesus Christ, who was I that could hinder God" (Acts 11:15, 17)?

Indeed, if the work of Christ on earth is the work of God, and if the work of the Spirit of Christ through the Holy Spirit, who could hinder God? If the same Holy Spirit that anoints males for leadership and pastoral ministry then anoints and sets apart females for the same leadership, who could hinder God? I argue that to refuse to recognize the work of Christ through the contemporary operation of the Holy Spirit might well be hindering the Work of God.

Recent hermeneutical theory has largely concentrated upon

the one, biblical narrative, though as Anthony Thiselton has suggested, attempting to maintain the "Two Horizons" of first century biblical time and our present time. My response is that the hermeneutical issue is not between the two horizons bracketed by the same Scripture text, but between the "two narratives." One narrative is the Scripture text, which does have two horizons, one original and one contemporary. The two narratives are both contemporary, in a sense, assuming that the contemporary text of Scripture is a faithful rendering of the original. Along with the contemporary Scripture narrative text is the narrative text of the work of the Holy Spirit. By saying that the Work of Christ interprets the Word of Christ, I am speaking of these two narratives, distinguished as a canonical and inspired text of Word of God and a non-canonical narrative of the contemporary work of Christ through the Holy Spirit.

"What do you think," was a favorite gambit of Jesus. "What do you think, Simon? From whom do kings of the earth take tribute? From their children or from others?" (Matt. 17:25; see also, 18:12; 21:28; 22:42). In each case, Jesus sought to draw his listeners into an inner logic contained within a life situation which revealed a truth concerning the nature and purpose of God

A word of caution. What I am saying is not to be construed as arguing for equal revelatory status of the two narratives. I hold the Scripture narrative to be the infallible and only source of revelation as Word of God. At the same time, the Scripture text says that Word of God has a purpose and an effect which must be recognized and read so as to receive Word of God. I then hold that the contemporary narrative text of the Work of Christ through the Holy Spirit must be interpreted as at least one form of the "purpose" for which Word of God is sent (Isaiah 55:11).

Let me give another example. I once participated in a debate sponsored by students over the issue of divorce and remarriage. My counterpart in the debate argued his position strongly. It was absolutely impossible to permit the remarriage of a divorced person on the grounds that Jesus forbad it by his teaching. Even the so-called "exception clause" in Matt. 19:9—"except for unchastity"—he argued was a later addition to the teachings of Jesus. There could be no exception, he stated, because the word of Jesus was final.

I had argued, based on my own pastoral experience, that a woman who had been divorced many years ago came to me as her pastor asking this question. "I was not the innocent party to the divorce, but I have confessed my sin and have received assurance of Christ's forgiveness and presence in my life. Pastor, you know the man with whom I am now in love as he attends this church and is part of our fellowship. He is a man who has also been divorced but along with me, has experienced the forgiveness and healing of Christ. We feel that Christ is present in our lives and in our love for each other. But I also know what the Bible says and from this I have been taught that I can never remarry as this would constitute adultery. But Pastor, on which side is God, is God on the side of the Bible or is God on our side in our new relationship in Christ?"

Faced with that question, I could only respond by saying that God was indeed present in their lives as the Spirit of Christ was clearly at work in renewing their lives in grace. On that basis I performed their marriage.

In recounting this as a narrative text of God's grace and as a criterion for interpreting the narrative text of Scripture as a basis for pastoral ministry, my opponent in the debate never wavered in his view.

Finally, a student raised his hand and asked: "Professor, you say that the sin of divorce, while it can be forgiven, allows for no remarriage; is that correct?" The answer was yes. "Then is it not also true that in the case of the death of one's spouse the surviving spouse could remarry as that would not violate the teaching of Jesus?" Again, the response was affirmative. I quickly saw where the good Professor was being led, and remained silent as the lamb was led to slaughter!

"Then what about this," the student asked, "in our city there was a pastor who became angry with his wife and shot and killed her. When he gets out of prison, is he now free to remarry seeing that instead of divorcing his wife he killed her?"

It was too late. The branch had been sawed off, and the Professor, consistent with his formal logic to the end, had to admit that, "yes, this man could remarry!" The laughter of the students over the absurdity of this case reduced his argument to folly, in their eyes. He, of course, while expressing deep discomfort over the logical outcome of his position, remained unmoved.

I return now to the discussion with which this chapter began. The pastors with whom I had argued my case were intrigued and interested. Their hesitation came with the matter of discernment of that which was genuinely a work of God through the Holy Spirit as the continuing ministry of Christ. How does one make this discernment, if indeed it can (and must!) be made?

Does every claim to be led of the Spirit of Christ have equal merit as a hermeneutical criterion? The answer is no. Returning again to the way in which the two narratives were correlated within the biblical text we find that for the Apostle Paul as well as for Jesus, there was always a biblical antecedent for what presented itself as a creative and liberating work of the Spirit. For example, with regard to the issue of circumcision, Paul did not simply replace the law of circumcision, nor the law of Moses, for that matter, with a new law of the Spirit. It was not the Holy Spirit that made an end of the law, but Christ (Romans 10:4). Paul had the narrative text of the Holy Spirit as the Spirit of Christ coming upon uncircumcised Gentiles. Now he looked back into the Scripture narrative for an antecedent to which he could link the narrative of the Spirit's work. He found it in Abraham, who was declared righteous by God before he was circumcised (Romans 4). Consequently, Paul placed the Scriptural narrative of the law as given by Moses into a temporary though purposeful context when he argued his case to the Galatian Christians. "The law [of Moses] was our disciplinarian [pedagogue] until Christ came. . . " (Gal. 3:24). Paul did not see this clearly until the narrative of Christ's Spirit coming upon the uncircumcised forced him to see it.

In the same way, while Paul adhered to the Scriptural narrative so far as it was useful in evangelizing both Jews and Gentiles as well as in pastoral care of the churches, he left several pointers to the narrative of the anointing of women for leadership in the church. While he permitted the circumcision of Timothy (Acts 16:3) out of expediency, he refused to have Titus circumcised (Gal. 2:3) as a sign of liberation from this historical and physical sign of membership in the covenant community. While he apparently restricted the role of women in the church at Ephesus (1 Tim. 2) he openly acknowledged the ministry of Lydia in the church at Philippi, of Phoebe, a <u>diakonos</u>, and Junia (apparently a woman) who was "prominent among the apostles" (Rom. 16:1, 7).

Circumcision, the subordination of women to men, and the legal requirements of the law all had precedent in the Scriptural narrative. It was the concept of Scriptural precedent that determined to a large degree the opposition of the religious leaders to the ministry of Jesus as well as to that of the Apostle Paul. Without consideration of the narrative of the work of God, the narrative of Word of God takes precedence. However, when the narrative of the work of God's Spirit through Jesus Christ is taken into account, we are now dealing with what I have called an "eschatological preference." That is to say, the Holy Spirit is a contemporary work of the coming Christ, as I have said earlier. Thus, the Spirit of the coming Christ already at work in the contemporary narrative provides a hermeneutical clue to the antecedent for such a work in the Scriptural narrative. Without such an antecedent, we cannot allow for what might be claimed as a new work of the Spirit to become a hermeneutical criterion.

That there are two narratives, I am convinced. The first narrative presents itself to us in Scripture as the Word of God written. The Scripture is the authoritative narrative with regard to inspired Word of God and revelation. The second narrative is a contemporary account of the work of the Holy Spirit as the contemporary presence and power of the resurrected Christ who is already coming into the world through the eschatological reality of Holy Spirit. This second narrative presents us with the hermeneutical significance of the Holy Spirit as the Work of Christ interprets the Word of Christ.

I have suggested two such narratives in the case of the role of women in pastoral leadership in the church and the case of pastoral ministry to those who have experienced divorce and seek God's grace for remarriage. The second narrative comes into play as we seek to discern the purpose of Word of God through the Work of God in specific situations which requires us to make decisions in concrete ministry situations. This is in accord with the teaching of Word of God itself, which urges us to discern not only the nature of Word of God as divine revelation but also the purpose of Word of God as it is proclaimed and taught (Isaiah 55:11).

Through this praxis of the Work of Christ through the Holy Spirit the Christ who was raised from the dead continues to express his will and desire for the restoration of humanity in reading and applying Word of Christ thoughtfully and obediently. Think about it!

4

Will Judas Be in Heaven?

"Do you think Judas will be in heaven?"

The man who asked me that question sat manacled to the table in Los Angeles County Jail, sentenced to life without parole for the brutal killing of his mother and father. He carried in his hands an underlined copy of a book I had written about Judas which had been given him by one of the volunteer chaplains.

"Can Judas really be forgiven for what he did? I did something worse than Judas, but somehow I believe that if there is hope for him there may be hope for me."

We talked for an hour. He wondered how Jesus could ever forgive Judas and whether what he himself had done might finally be unforgivable, even by God. He pursued the question to the point where I finally said, "Let me ask you a question. Suppose that when you die God confronts you with your parents whom you murdered and tells them that they now have the power to make a determination as to your eternal destiny. These are the parents whom you murdered. What will they say?"

He paused for a long while and finally said slowly, "My mother will forgive me, for she loved me, I am sure of that." To which I replied, "Then you know that God can forgive you, for he has taken upon himself your guilt through the death and resurrection of Christ."

Difficult as it was for him to internalize the reality of God's forgiveness, the case of Judas became a door through which he could walk.

I began musing about Judas years ago. It began with a sermon I preached in the middle 1960s titled "Judas as an Answer to Prayer." After praying all night, Jesus then called all of his disciples and out of them chose the twelve including, as Luke records it, "Judas Iscariot, who became a traitor" (Luke 6:16). I pondered the significance of that choice in light of the night spent in prayer. One could well assume that the purpose of the night spent in prayer was to seek divine guidance in the choosing of the twelve. I will leave for another time some reflections on what this might say about prayer in our own lives. For Jesus, it certainly enabled him to accept even the betrayal by Judas at the end as bracketed by his prayer which placed all of life and destiny in the hands of the Father.

The thought of Judas being in heaven is what triggered the request from the prisoner to talk with me. As a convicted murderer, who did not deny the act, he now thought of his life beyond death and what it would mean to face the judgment of God for his act.

I presented this encounter as a case for discussion with my seminary students. There was general agreement that if the prisoner had confessed the sin of murder and trusted Christ for forgiveness he could be assured of eternal life with God in heaven. While some questioned the authenticity of such a conversion under these circumstances, it was agreed that only God knows the heart and that there is always some degree of ambiguity in the human profession of faith, especially when it has not yet been tested as to its endurance and growth. We were reminded of the conversion of Carla Faye Tucker, the woman in Texas who had participated in a terrible crime of murder and only later in prison under sentence of death did she accept Christ as savior and profess a transformation of life. In her case several years passed by before she was executed during which she taught Bible classes in prison and demonstrated a consistent testimony to a new life in Christ.

Even the brother of one of the victims affirmed the genuineness of her conversion and, himself being a Christian, expressed confidence that she was forgiven by God and is now in heaven after her execution.

Setting aside the ambiguity regarding the prisoner with whom I had my conversation, the theological issue in our discussion of this case emerged when I raised the matter of the victims of this man's murder, his own parents. Assuming that his parents had given no evidence or indication of their faith in Christ prior to their death, is it possible that their son, the murderer, would go to heaven based on his conversion to Christ while his parents would end up in hell?

Some students agreed, though reluctantly, that this indeed would be the case assuming that they had no opportunity to repent and receive Christ as savior before their murder. Their response was determined by the conviction that only those who personally accept Christ in this life can be saved. Furthermore, some added, the idea that Judas could be in heaven was itself an unwarranted assumption given the fact that he not only betrayed Jesus but also committed suicide. One's eternal destiny is determined by one's relationship to Christ and this must take place before death. Otherwise, they said, what motive would there be for taking the gospel of Christ to the unsaved?

Other students were offended by this, saying that it would be outrageous for God to save the murderer while sending the victims to hell. When pressed, they had no basis for their feelings other than it "just didn't seem right!"

My own musings on this issue cause me to reflect upon how theologians in the past might respond to my case scenario. Calvin would no doubt respond by reminding us that the eternal destiny of every human person is determined by the decree of God prior to the creation of the world. "All things being at God's disposal," wrote Calvin "and the decision of salvation or death belonging to him, he orders all things by his counsel and decree in such a manner, that some men are born devoted from the womb to certain death, that his name may be glorified in their destruction" (*Institutes.*, III, 23, 6). In other words, Calvin held that every person is predestined by God to either salvation or reprobation (hell) by the sovereign decree of God. It is not the human act of repentance and faith that determines salvation, but God alone, and that apart from any subjective human response. In effect, the death of Christ on the cross did not alter the number of persons ultimately destined for either heaven or hell by so much as one.

Calvin would warn us not to assume that the son by his contrition, remorse and faith could alter the divine decree concerning his eternal destiny. If God had indeed predestined him for eternal life then the son could not change that even by his heinous act of murder. If in fact, he did express repentance and faith in Christ this may have been the work of God's Spirit to make efficacious in his life what God had already predestined in his case. So also with regard to the parents, Calvin would remind us. Their apparent lack of saving faith would in itself not disannul their eternal salvation if God had predestined them for salvation. In other words, we really do not know and must bow before the sovereignty of God rather than to speculate. Because we do not know, Calvin would say, we should offer the gospel to all so that God's predestination can produce faith where it has been determined for those elect to salvation. For those not elect to salvation, even their profession of faith, as in the case of the son, would have no eternal significance.

Calvin, or course had his own pastoral concerns when it came to assurance of salvation. If our eternal destiny depends upon the genuineness of our subjective repentance and faith, then we would always be cast back upon the weakness of our faith and the subjective doubts about our repentance as a sufficient condition for forgiveness. Assuming that our faith, weak though it may be, is produced in our hearts by the inward witness of the Holy Spirit, then we can have confidence that we are the elect due to God's own decree and his sovereign will.

When applied to this particular case, Calvin's solution to the problem raised as much consternation as it brought comfort. For those who accepted Calvin's theory of predestination, it seemed to resolve the issue at the intellectual level. Whatever feelings one had about the possible unfairness of such an arrangement were to be set aside, as Calvin himself suggested, citing the Apostle Paul's statement, "But who indeed are you, a human being, to argue with God? Will what is molded say to the one who molds it, 'Why have you made me like this?' Has the potter no right over the clay, to make out of the same lump one object for special use and another for ordinary use" (Romans 9:20,21)?

Jacobus Arminius, a generation later than Calvin, could not accept the relentless logic of Divine predestination. Arguing for the freedom of human will, despite the sinful condition of the human heart, Arminius placed the ultimate responsibility for one's eternal destiny upon each person's decision for or against Christ after hearing the Gospel. According to Arminius, the doctrine of divine predestination and election as taught by Calvin is "repugnant to the nature of God" (who is merciful and just), "contrary to the nature of man" (who has freedom of the will), "injurious to the glory of God," and "dishonorable to Jesus Christ our Savior."

If we were to ask Arminius to comment on the scenario above, he would encourage us to believe that the son who murdered his parents could truly be forgiven by God through repentance and faith in Christ. If he truly exercised freedom of will to receive the grace of Christ while still alive, he could well have been pardoned by God and received in to heaven.

As to the parents, however, the ambiguity of their relation with God due to lack of evidence of saving faith in Christ, creates a barrier to further speculation. Doubtless Arminius would say what many pastors who follow in his tradition are forced to speak words of comfort at the graveside to those who grieve without placing the departed in heaven—We commit the soul of this loved one to his Creator with confidence that the judge of all the earth will do right. In other words, believe what you will or what you need about the eternal destiny of your loved one, just don't ask me to justify it theologically.

This, of course, leaves us with the tormenting question with which we began this inquiry—is it possible that the murderer will be in heaven while his victims go to hell because they did not have the same opportunity that he had to receive and believe the gospel?

The debate between Calvin and Arminius concerning divine sovereignty and human free will has never been resolved by theologians. The scenario I have presented only serves to tease out the inherent problems with each, leaving pastors caught on the horns of a theological dilemma.

The modern theologian, Karl Barth, was not unaware of this and suggested a totally different approach. Barth did not begin (as Calvin did) with abstract concepts concerning divine sovereignty and the decrees of double predestination, nor (as Arminius did) with human concepts of free will and individual choice. Rather, Barth began with God's act of self revelation in Jesus Christ as the only source of our knowledge of God's actions with regard to the human situation and eternal destiny. As the incarnate Son of God, Barth argued that Jesus assumed on behalf of all humans both the fatal separation from God caused by sin and the hopeful promise of reconciliation through his own death and resurrection.

If one must speak of election and predestination, Barth argued, then we can only see this as determined and fulfilled through Jesus Christ as the elect one, both to reprobation and to salvation. The threefold act of God, understood theologically as the trinity, can now be understood as follows. God the Father is the Creator of the world and humankind, loving the world and not willing that any should perish (John 3:16). God the Son is the Reconciler of all humanity through his incarnate life, death and resurrection, taking upon himself the consequence of sin so that the world may be reconciled to God (2 Cor. 5:18-19). God the Holy Spirit is the Redeemer, who awakens those "dead in sin" to new life in Christ.

Consequently, Paul says of himself, "I have been crucified with Christ; and it is no longer I who live, but it is Christ who lives in me. And the life I now live in the flesh I live by faith in the Son of God, who loved me and gave himself for me" Galatians 2:19-20). All human beings have been crucified with Christ, whether they know it or not. But not every human being can say with Paul, nonetheless, "it is no longer I who live, but it is Christ who lives in me." Barth has reminded us that the death and resurrection of Christ did not redeem all humanity, but created in Christ the objective basis of reconciliation between God and humanity. It is the Holy Spirit who redeems persons through the spiritual transformation from death to life: "So if anyone is in Christ, there is a new creation: everything old has passed away; see, everything has become new!" (2 Corinthians 5:17). If anyone does not have the Spirit of Christ that person does not belong to Christ (Ro. 8:9).

Does this mean that all humans, being reconciled to God are therefore redeemed? No, says Barth. What it does mean is that God has taken upon himself the fate of eternal estrangement and so removed death as an obstacle to the possibility of redemption of all. Will all be eventually redeemed asks Barth? Not necessarily, he argues, for this would be to presume upon God's freedom. We can think out theologically what God has revealed to us through Christ, but we cannot speculate beyond that which is revealed in Christ. God is not under some logical necessity to redeem all evil, says Barth. There can never be a time when God surrenders his freedom to some "inner necessity" of his being to satisfy our logical demand for an answer.

So what does this mean with regard to the scenario described above? As far as Barth is concerned, we are left with both a promise and a warning. The promise is that God has destroyed the power of death to determine eternal destiny for human beings through the resurrection of Christ. It is not death that determines our eternal destiny but God. And the God who will sit in judgment of all after death is Christ himself. All must appear before the judgment seat of Christ following death, says the Apostle Paul (2 Cor. 5:10). The warning is not to speculate or predetermine what God might achieve with regard to actual redemption of those for whom Christ has reconciled through his own death and resurrection. If some humans are finally judged to be irredeemably evil, that remains for Christ to determine.

In presenting this case to my students I pressed the point of the final judgment where Christ will render the decision with regard to every person. Is the verdict already determined before Christ assumes the seat of judgment? Calvin would, of course say, yes; Christ cannot but dispense the judgment already determined by divine predestination. Arminius, would also assent, on different grounds. Those who do not exercise their free will to receive Christ before death have sealed their fate. It only remains for the verdict to be read.

But is it not possible that the judgment rendered by Christ will be an actual decision or determination grounded in the freedom of God? Is it not possible that the judgment of Christ will be an actual determination rather than simply reading the verdict already determined? If so, then there remains after death a final determination of one's eternal destiny, surely taking into account one's life before death, but not totally determined by that.

Evangelical theologian Donald Bloesch suggests that those who have died without having an opportunity to accept Christ will then have that chance: "Salvation is fixed at death for those who are in Christ, but the condemnation of those who have never known about Christ is not decided at death. . . . I affirm not the doctrine of a second chance for salvation after death but the universality of a first chance. Those who were unable to hear the gospel in this life will surely be given such an opportunity in the Word of Spirit."

Bloesch would thus respond to the scenario by suggesting that the parents who were murdered by their son may well have the same opportunity as the son to receive the good news of Jesus Christ. What Bloesch has done is to push the

Arminian position of human free will beyond death as a way of resolving the tormenting question posed in our case scenario. The suggestion by Bloesch appears as a fragment of his own "musing" without any theological basis offered.

What Barth has offered, whether or not one agrees, is a solid theological argument for the freedom of God to make a final determination of human destiny not based on a theory of predestination (Calvin) nor upon human free will (Arminius), but upon God's own act through Jesus Christ by which the power of death to determine human destiny has been once and for all overcome through the death and resurrection of God's own Son, Jesus Christ.

Barth leaves us with no clear answer to the question of the eternal destiny of both the son who murdered his parents and the parents who were the victim. Instead, Barth points us to the threefold work of God as outlined above. The work of God the Father has resulted in the incarnation of the Son as a vicarious representation of all humanity. This is in accord with the Apostle Paul's analogy in which he states that through the first man, Adam, death as a result of sin is the condition of all humanity while life has come to all through the grace of the one man, Jesus Christ (Romans 5:12-17). The work of the Son through death and resurrection has resulted in the reconciliation of the world to God, whereby God no longer "counts trespasses against them" (2 Cor. 5:18-19). The work of the Holy Spirit creates a new nature in those who are transformed from "death to life" in Jesus Christ. It is this work of the Spirit that may well continue beyond death, not merely human free will.

So, will Judas be in heaven? Not really. That is, not the Judas who is the betrayer, but possibly a "born anew" Judas through the power of the Holy Spirit in the encounter with Christ which occurs after death (2 Cor. 5:10). Will Ray Anderson be in heaven? Not the Ray Anderson who is "dead in trespasses and sins" (Eph. 2:2) but a "born anew" Ray Anderson through the power of the Holy Spirit, of which I have present assurance of a future reality, the "pledge of our inheritance" (Eph. 1:13-14). Both Judas and I will appear before the final judgment seat of Christ. I "fear no condemnation" (Rom. 8:1), and I would like to think that this fear will also be removed in the case of Judas.

The man who murdered his parents will meet them again at the judgment seat of Christ. Thank God it is the same Jesus Christ who was an advocate for the condemned, estranged and yes, victims of the sins of others, who will make the final decision. Is this not good news? Think about it!

5

What Do I Say At the Graveside of a Suicide?

I was once asked to officiate at the graveside service of a young mother who, on a bright and sunny spring day, dropped off her youngest daughter at her husband's place of work and inexplicably went home to take her own life. The family members were stunned and stricken with grief and remorse. "Why could we have not seen that she was suffering so much?" they asked. "Yes, she had some problems, but she seemed to be coping with them well enough."

I discovered that she was noted for her beautiful garden and her love for flowers. Lovely vases filled with fresh flowers could be found in every part of her home. At the graveside service, I commented on that, and said something like this: "Peggy herself [not her real name] appeared to be a beautiful vase. Yet from the inside, she saw her life as cracked and falling to pieces if she let go of it. Nor could she hand it over to someone else to hold for her, for it took both hands to keep it together, and if she even took one hand off to ask for assistance, she feared it would fall apart. What we saw was a beautiful person, like a vase, with imperfections to be sure, but with no fatal flaws. What she saw from the inside were fractures which never could be mended. Her life broke from the inside out. Only in this tragic end do we feel her pain as a bond with her and with God. His grace is now her healing and our comfort."

I went on to suggest that only she could crawl into that broken vase of her life where we were helpless to enter. But the message of the Christian gospel is that God sent his Son Jesus not only to enter into human life at its strongest but also at its weakest. Jesus not only stood with those who were sick and in despair but he entered into the soul of human brokenness at the hour of their most desperate aloneness. Hidden from us, and perhaps from her as well, Jesus was there with her in the fractured vase of her life.

Jesus was with us there at the graveside of a suicide.

We are living in days in which apparently healthy persons deliberately take their own lives rather than face the fears of an uncertain future. The increasing incidence of suicide among teenagers shocks us into the recognition that the insulation which protects our society from the terror of meaninglessness has become frayed and worn thin. Behind the shining faces of our children lie the skeletons of ancient fears for which our world of science and technology has no comfort. Beneath the surface of success flows the torrent of an untamed river which seeks to suck us into the vortex of future shock. It is as though we have no present, only the rapidly receding past and the onrushing future which only promises more isolated weariness and fragmented pleasure.

The desire for life, inherent at birth, is sustained by most of us despite sometimes enormous discouragement and pain. For some, the thoughts of suicide are random whispers which lack substance, like images of a bad dream that disappear when exposed to the waking hours of daylight. For others, these become nagging voices begging consideration as the "final solution" to daytime life which has become a living nightmare.

This inborn desire for life can grow weak under the layers of accumulated living where the burden of life becomes greater than its beauty. When thoughts of suicide become an insistent obsession, the desire for life must be repressed even further. One cannot entertain both notions, that of desiring to live while also intending to die. The desire to live must be silenced in order to focus the self on the intention to die.

I have conducted graveside services for more than one person who chose suicide as a final solution. I have talked with some who have tried and failed. I have talked with many who think about suicide, some seemingly obsessed with the idea. But no one has ever talked with one who actually took his or her own life—no one has come back to tell us what the final motivation was, what made the intention a final act. Even with Peggy, one can only guess what drove her to this desperate and tragic conclusion.

One might call the suicidal impulse or obsession a sickness unto death, like a condition which attacks the immune system of one's vital life force. But it is a sickness of the soul, a twisted and distorted version of life that becomes a compelling vision of death. For those who attempt to prevent it, it appears as the ultimate insanity. For those who attempt it, I suspect that it becomes the only passageway of sanity in a world and life gone insane.

There may be, in the thought of suicide, a simplicity which seems to offer a light at the end of the tunnel, a way to transform life's vexations into a vision of escape. The logic of self annihilation becomes inexorable, its wisdom brilliant, its outcome peace. It can be a powerful argument against the logic of living when the battleground is the psyche of the one immersed in despair. For each person's life has its own logic, and the reasonableness of another's is senseless to our own, when we are pushed to extremity.

When faced with the inexplicable act of suicide, some have attempted to explain it by viewing such an act as the inevitable consequence of that person's sin. One might even find support for such despair by reading the biblical account of the human dilemma as though divine judgment were the final word. But this would be to miss the main theme of the biblical witness to God's grace, where the final word is not judgment but mercy.

On one occasion, a disciple of Jesus inquired about a man born blind from birth, "Rabbi, who sinned, this man or his parents, that he was born blind?" (John 9:2) For the disciples, this was a perfectly logical question! They no doubt had been warned by their parents and instructed by the synagogue teachers to avoid the consequences of sin by being careful not to violate the law of God. "It is only the person who sins that shall die. . . ."(Ezekiel 18:4).

When this logic of cause and effect has been drummed into the mind by teachers and used by parents to frighten a child into performance acceptable enough to earn their praise, one develops a conscience rooted in fear of condemnation. If one could reason backwards from the evidence of God's judgment to the sin that caused that judgment it might seem logical and simple as long as it happens to someone else!

I have no hesitation in saying that this is sick psychology and bad theology! There is a better psychology and a worthier theology when we view our lives from God's perspective. It was sin that produced the deep sense of shame which Adam and Eve felt and which led them to conceal themselves from the other and from God. The healing touch of God upon their lives removed that shame and restored their self image even as it restored them to relationship with each other. It is the grace of God which transforms our inner life from self disgust to self worth. It is the love of God which empowers us to love ourselves in order that we might then love others.

From the very beginning, God intervened and the terrible logic of sin and death was broken before it had a chance to claim its first victims. Adam and Eve both sinned, but did not die. Instead, they were restored to life out of death through divine intervention. God pointed to the terrible consequence of sin when he warned, "in the day that you eat of it you shall die" (Gen 2:17). This death as separation from God goes beyond the physical death which is natural to all creatures, including the human, taken from the dust of the ground. Under the torment of this death as separation from God's life, the self suffers both psychologically and spiritually long before physical death occurs. The consequences are real and terrible in their power to destroy.

But our spiritual state is not determined by the consequences of sin but by the counsel of God. "I have no pleasure in the death of any one, says the Lord God; turn then, and live" (Ezekiel 18:32). God stands between us and the consequences of sin, with his law in one hand and forgiveness in the other.

The self can become its own prosecuting attorney and builds a file of evidence against which there is no defense. Justice, not mercy, is the demand of law. The self may seek mercy, but when the self is also the accuser, the trial is short and the judgment swift. When the dialogue stays within our own minds, sin quickly turns to sickness of soul, for which there is no forgiveness. Forgiveness requires some word from the other who is the one sinned against.

John [not his real name] was in excellent physical health when he died. A successful engineer, and unmarried, he struggled from loneliness and suffered through the breaking up of an unsatisfactory relationship. He appeared to find consolation in his relationship with God, but then he was discovered dead in his car, with an open Bible lying beside him. He had taken his own life.

As a pastor I was expected to interpret his tragic death to grief stricken survivors. A member of the church challenged me for providing a Christian burial service: "This man placed himself outside of God's grace by taking his own life."

Is this true? Is suicide different from other kinds of death? Is death by one's own hand a death that is not included in the saving significance of the death of Christ? What of a child who unknowingly drinks a poisonous substance and subsequently dies? We are told that this was an accident, not a suicide, for though death was by the child's own hand it was not by the child's deliberate intention.

It seems that it is not death itself, even death by one's own hand, which places one outside of God's grace—if indeed this is possible! It is the intention which is the fatal sin. In this view, suicide is not only morally wrong but it is a sin against God for which there is no grace, no forgiveness, because the death removes the possibility of repentance. But if this were true, one would be as guilty for an unsuccessful attempt at suicide as for a successful one. But then, so the argument goes, one is granted a reprieve and so can repent and find grace from God.

The Judeo-Christian tradition through the ages has not been kind to the one who commits suicide. Suicide was generally considered as a *felo de se*, or as a crime against one's own self. In fact, in Britain it was considered a crime up to the passing of the Suicide Act of 1961. Even under this law, it remains an offense to assist a suicide. In the United States, suicide is still a crime in many states. During the medieval period, the Church often refused to bury the victim of a suicide in the "sacred" burial grounds surrounding the church. To this day, many are uneasy about disposing of the remains of a person who has committed suicide, perhaps feeling that even the corpse represents some kind of offense to God.

The fact that suicide might be considered an unforgivable sin is based on a perspective of life which holds that one's relationship with God and one's existing in a stage of grace is somehow dependent upon the fragile connection which is sustained by one's own volition. The German theologian, Dietrich Bonhoeffer, wrote that suicide is a specifically human act, because it issues out of the freedom which human beings possess. This freedom is not an absolute freedom and right over one's own life, to dispose of as one wishes. Rather, it is a freedom of life and death before God. Many people have died without repenting of their sins, Bonhoeffer wrote. To make repentance a condition by which the grace of God is received is "setting too much store by the last moment of life."

If we are to find some theological basis for understanding the implications for a death by one's own hand we must first of all understand that the death of any human being, by whatever means, is the same kind of death. Human death is more than a natural end to mortal life; it is also a consequence of sin and a fatal spiritual estrangement from God. The consequence of sin is spiritual death, not merely that humans became guilty and only needed forgiveness. "The wages of sin is death," wrote Paul (Ro. 6:23). This kind of death entered into humanity by the act of our original parents, Adam and Eve, argued Paul. This death is the same death that was assumed by God in becoming human in order that "through death he might destroy the one who has the power of death, that is the devil, and free those who all their lives were held in slavery by the fear of death" (Heb. 2:14-15).

A few years ago I was asked to speak at a memorial service for one of my students, who had served as my teaching assistant, and who had taken his own life without leaving any kind of note or explanation for this terrible and shocking act. All death is the same, I said. Death by one's own hand is not a different kind of death. It is death that represents the great human dilemma due to the fall of the human race from spiritual life with God.

Death has been destroyed as having the power to determine human destiny through the death and resurrection of Christ. No longer can we ever say that how one dies, or even the fact that one dies, determines our eternal destiny. It is God who makes that final determination, and the God who makes that determination is one known to us, Jesus Christ (2 Cor. 5:10). Whatever caused this young man to take his own life, we do not comfort ourselves by attributing psychological reasons so as to excuse the act. We have better theological grounds to place his death by his own hand, under the consequence of sin which has been removed once and for all through the resurrection of Christ. This is gospel, not grief counseling.

Beyond the theological considerations of a suicide, I continue to ponder the effect of death by suicide upon the human psyche. I have argued that death by one's own hand is not a different kind of death than death by any other means. At the same time, there seem to be other than theological reasons why the ancient church and many even today have a felt need to consider death by suicide to have crossed some boundary and transgressed not only a moral but a spiritual law.

If we are honest, we will admit to a psychic wound in the soul which goes beyond grief in hearing about the suicide of one close to us. There is a feeling that something almost sacred has been violated in such an act. Death causes a pain of loss and grief that often leaves us stricken with inexpressible sorrow. Suicide is more than death, it is a crack in the surface of life, life which each of us carries as a fragile vessel encasing the self.

As I groped for some way of entering into the abyss created in the lives of the young woman's husband, mother and close friends at her graveside service, I pictured her life as a beautiful vase which to others appeared to be virtually perfect. The fact that she collected such vases and arranged her outer life with such precision and beauty, gave me a clue to what it might have been like for her to live behind this porcelain facade. The more perfect we maintain the surface of the self, the more fragile it becomes.

Our own lives are like that to some extent. Even though we acknowledge the cracks and blemishes on the surface in some semblance of authenticity, each of us works hard to hold the surface together in order to "tame the terror of being alive," as Ernest Becker once put it in his prize winning book, <u>The Denial of Death</u>. Becker uses a literary scalpel to peel away the "character armor" that we build around the self in order to survive in a world that constantly threatens our mortality until he has exposed the deeper anxiety or dread which lies in the self. We have found ways to ritualize and routinize the death of others in most cases, as a way of repressing the deeper dread of our own mortality. When this becomes built up layer upon layer, we become virtually impervious to the destruction of this "armor" around the self. Even some cracks which appear in the outer layer do not reach through to the inner most layer. Thus we can handle loss and bear grief in a somewhat normal manner. Even the evidences of our own inevitable mortality can be repaired, as it were, by rituals of denial and projections of the immortality of the self.

I will always remember the almost supernatural feeling of well being and, yes, immortality I felt in driving away from the cemetery having conducted my first funeral service as a fledging pastor. The stark contrast between the grave which I had just left and the sense of power and aliveness at driving through the green and growing grass, flowers and life around me, was so exhilarating as to be intoxicating. Feeling guilty for such a quick release from the morbid reality of death, I censored myself and admitted that someday others would drive away from my own gravesite with more or less the same feelings. At the same time, I now realize that repair work had been done on the surface of my self and I could now enter back into life without a gnawing feeling of anxiety and dread.

Whether or not one has conscious feelings about death, to claim the promise and experience the reality of Christ deep within the self is a source of healing and hope. The Apostle Paul found this reality for himself and encouraged us to know "Christ in you, the hope of glory" (Col. 1:27). Perhaps we will always need some form of the character armor that shields us from the evidences of our mortality in everyday life. But we need not use this as a porcelain shell within which our love for self withers and dies. For "God's love has been poured into our hearts through the Holy Spirit that has been given to us" (Ro. 5:5). Think about it!

6

Did Jesus Have to Die on a Cross?

In a theological examination for a prospective faculty member, one of my colleagues posed this question to the candidate: "What work did Jesus accomplish on the cross for our salvation?" I wanted to interrupt and say, "Nothing! A dead man cannot do any work!" But I held my tongue, and the candidate plunged ahead, giving a traditional, and apparently, acceptable answer.

The traditional doctrine of the atonement is almost exclusively focused upon the death of Jesus on the cross as offering complete satisfaction for the dishonor done to God through human sin. The "work" of Christ, therefore, in this view is taken to be the offering up of his life as a sacrifice to fulfill divine justice and permit God to pardon freely all who accept death of Jesus as a substitute for their own death. This "passive obedience" is considered a work which Jesus accomplished in submitting to death. The forgiveness of sin is offered by God based on the satisfaction achieved by the death of Christ.

The candidate, I should add, provided exactly this kind of response and passed with flying colors, having guessed correctly what the question was meant to elicit. Wisely keeping quiet during the investigation of the candidate's theology, I carried over my concern into my class which followed the next day. It is usually safer to explore innovative theology with students than with faculty colleagues! This is true, even though sooner or later, the "cat is out of the bag," so to speak, and one must be prepared to give account of one's own theological convictions, even if they take the form of musings.

"If Jesus had died of a heart attack in the Garden of Gethsemane," I asked my students, "and the disciples carried him out and placed him in a tomb. Would there have been a resurrection?" Only a few hands went up. The rest were stunned by the thought and not prepared to respond.

Some who raised their hands argued that he would have been raised from the dead because he was the Son of God, irrespective of how he died. I then played my trump card. "Assuming that he would have been raised from the dead, would there have been an atonement. Could we still say that he died for our sins?"

Now I saw a flurry of hands, and the consensus was that, no, there could not have been an atonement because he did not die on the cross, shedding his blood to wash away our sins. My students too had learned the "correct answer."

Some refused to entertain the hypothesis, feeling that the question was itself irrelevant, if not blasphemous. "Jesus died on the cross in fulfillment of Scripture and as God had determined," one protested. "It couldn't have happened any other way."

At the same time, I could tell that there was growing discomfort with this conclusion. Other students were now beginning to do some theological reflection, and one responded, "It was the resurrection that counted anyway. Without a resurrection there would be no atonement, even if he died on the cross."

Amazing! Here was a student coming up with a theological insight I had never heard mentioned in the theological exam of the faculty candidate. I read from Paul's letter to the Corinthians, "If Christ has not been raised, your faith is futile and you are still in your sins. Then those also who have died in Christ have perished" (1 Cor. 15:17-18).

It is the resurrection of Jesus, not just his death on the cross, that completed the atonement, I went on to suggest.

The reason for this is that it is not just that sin that needs to be forgiven, but death that needs to be overcome. The consequence of sin is death as Adam and Eve were warned (Genesis 2:17).

Furthermore, if Jesus assumed a human nature subject to death in his conception and birth, then death was inevitable for him, regardless of the means. Yes, there was in retrospect, after the crucifixion of Jesus, ample evidence in Scripture that even the means of death has been foreseen by God. But death on a cross was not necessary, only that the death assumed by Jesus be completed and that he be raised from the dead in order that the atonement could be completed and humanity restored to fellowship with God.

Why is that so many of our songs and hymns focus on the cross and seldom on resurrection, and then only at Easter? Why is there a preoccupation with the "power of the blood" to wash away sin? Are we really saved by the blood of Jesus? Certainly the significance of blood is clearly portrayed in the Old Testament. The blood of animals was required for forgiveness of sins and without the shedding of blood there is no forgiveness of sins (Hebrews 9:22).

A clue as to the significance of blood is found in Leviticus 17:11, "For the life of the flesh is in the blood; and I have given it to you for making atonement for your lives on the altar; for, as life, it is the blood that makes atonement." Blood is understood to be "life blood," so that when an animal "bleeds to death," the blood becomes a token of the life of the animal given as a sacrifice. Because it is "impossible for the blood of bulls and goats to take away sins" (Hebrews 10:4), Christ gave his own life (blood) in taking upon himself the consequence of human sin. Thus the blood of Christ became a synonym for his life, given over to death on the cross.

It would be grotesque and preposterous to think that if one had a container of the blood of Jesus that it would represent some kind of merit or have any saving significance. It was the death that Jesus assumed in becoming human that he brought to completion on the cross. But it was in his resurrection that his death gained significance, for apart from resurrection, as the Apostle Paul clearly stated, there is no forgiveness of sin. In other words, apart from the resurrection of Jesus there was no atonement for sin, no salvation for sinners, no reconciliation between humans and God (1 Cor. 15:17).

Something seems to have gone awry in the church's traditional doctrine of the atonement which focused almost entirely upon the death of Jesus rather than his resurrection. For the first thousand years of the church's existence theologians by and large reflected upon the liberation of humans from bondage to sin through the life of Jesus as the divine Son of God. Some understood sin to be removed as a disease through the incarnation of God, infusing divine qualities of life into the corrupted body of humanity. Others viewed sin as a moral defect to be overcome through the divine moral quality of Jesus' person and life. Still others viewed sin as being held captive by Satan to be released from bondage through the victory of Jesus over death in the resurrection, in effect, ransoming humans from Satan's power. In all of these views, the purpose of the life, death and resurrection of Jesus was understood to have a primary effect upon humans.

With Anselm of Canterbury (1033-1109), a new perspective entered medieval soteriology. Anselm argued strongly against the classical ransom theory, saying that the debt owed was not to Satan but to God, for the dishonor which sin had done to him. According to Anselm, the sinner is held fast by a duty to bring satisfaction of a penal nature. Only the perfect humanity of Christ (who has no debt of his own) can make this payment. Anselm wrote:

> This is the debt which man and angel owe to God, and no one who pays this debt commits sin... and this is the sole and complete debt of honor which we owe to God... He who does not render this honor which is due to God, robs God of his own and dishonors him; and this is sin.... For God will not do it, because he has no debt to pay; and man will not do it, because he cannot. Therefore, in order that the God-man may perform this, it is necessary that the same

being should be perfect God and perfect man, in order to make this atonement.

For the first time, the primary effect of the life and death of Jesus was considered to be on God, not on humans. It was God, Anselm argued, who needed to be satisfied before he could offer pardon and forgiveness.

The satisfaction theory was also part of Calvin's theory of the atonement, as well as the other Reformers. The purpose of the death of Christ, said Calvin, was "to discharge the debts due from others, and thereby to obtain a righteousness for them....For if Christ had not made a satisfaction for our sins, he could not be said to have appeased God by suffering punishment to which we were exposed."

Abelard (1079-1144), a contemporary of Anselm, was outraged by the suggestion that God needed to be satisfied by the death of an innocent man in order to feel free to offer forgiveness and pardon. "Indeed, how cruel and wicked it seems that anyone should demand the blood of an innocent person as the price for anything, or that it should in any way please him that an innocent man should be slain—still less that God should consider the death of his Son so agreeable that by it he should be reconciled to the world."

Five centuries later, Socinus (1509-1604) could be equally blunt: "Why should God have willed to kill his innocent Son by a cruel and execrable death, when there was no need of satisfaction? In this way both the generosity of the Son perishes, and, instead of a most benign and munificent God, with supreme impiety and unspeakable sacrilege, we concoct for ourselves a God who is base and sordid."

Contemporary theologians also find Anselm's concept of satisfaction troubling. Otto Weber complains, "But the fact remains that Anselm constructs 'satisfaction' abstractly, as an a priori. This is the result of his realism. But that does not make it right... Anselm gives a peculiarly unsure answer to the question as to how 'satisfaction' affects man." H. D. McDonald echoes this criticism when he says: "Anselm has in fact built his theory of atonement on a view of God other than he himself has affirmed, for his theory is based on the analogy of God as a medieval sovereign quick to react to affronts to his personal dignity. But that is not an adequate guide to an understanding of Christ's work."

The root of the problem is Anselm's theory concerning how sin affects God and how God proposes to remove it by the sacrifice of his innocent Son in order to "satisfy" his justice. Despite elements in Anselm's treatment of the atonement with which we can find agreement, the failure to root the atonement ultimately in the resurrection of Christ skews his treatment of the subject. As a result, the cross became the focal point rather than resurrection.

One must surely say that it was not the death of Jesus the Son which satisfied God the Father, but his resurrection from the dead! It is life that God desires, not death. Even if Jesus had bled to death, this would not have removed sin and restored relation to God. In being raised from the dead, the death of Jesus could then be understood as necessary in order that the consequence of sin, which is death, be assumed by God's very self and its power over humans be destroyed. The "sting of death" is removed not by dying, but in victory over death though resurrection, argues Paul (1 Cor. 15:56-57).

How important is it that we have a better understanding of atonement than Anselm? Does it really matter whether we have our primary focus on removal of guilt through the death of Jesus or the restoration of life through union with the resurrected Christ? In my pastoral experience it matters a great deal.

When the primary focus of our salvation is grounded in the forensic, or legal, act of forgiveness as a result of satisfaction to God's sense of justice, we have assurance that guilt is removed as an objective offense against God, but not the sense of shame which affects our inner self. C. Norman Kraus argues that the traditional approach has dealt almost exclusively with the relation of the cross to guilt, as the moral and legal basis for removal of a penalty. The atonement must also be seen, argues Kraus, as effective in dealing with shame as well as with guilt. The intention of atonement, says Kraus is not first of all to placate a wrathful God but to overcome the consequence of sin both in its objective and subjective nature. The atonement "must deal with the intrinsic consequences of guilt—both its internal and external consequences, and it must do this in such a way that it does not condone or augment the objective fault. The intention of forgiveness is to nullify shame and guilt so that reconciliation and a new beginning become possible. The shamed person must find new identity and personal worth."

Far too many Christians with whom I have come into contact both personally and pastorally continue to suffer from spiritual and emotional unhealth, which assurance of pardon from the guilt of sin does not heal. If God is satisfied, many people who accept God's forgiveness as a legal pardon are not.

Most churches incorporate some form of confession of sin and the granting of absolution as part of their liturgy and worship. This corporate confession of sin is often followed immediately by the granting of absolution, without making any attempt to see that the effects of sin are removed from the person's life. Too often the granting of absolution as assurance of the forgiveness of sins is little more than a legal transaction. When the church pronounces forgiveness of sins and spiritual peace with God without also providing the power to overcome the effect of sins in one's daily life, this may not only be a liturgical fraud but spiritual malpractice! Let me explain.

Suppose a man went to a medical doctor for a diagnosis concerning a pain in some part of his body, and was told there was a malignant tumor that could cause death. Before leaving the office, after some massage and manipulation, the man was told by the doctor that he was now completely healed based upon his authority as a medical professional, and needed no further treatment. When the man died of cancer only a few weeks later, would not the doctor be liable for charges of malpractice?

In somewhat the same way, if sin is a condition which affects our personal life and leads to death (the wages of sin is death), then assurance that forgiveness has been granted without removing the effect of the sin would be equivalent to spiritual malpractice. Why are we uncomfortable with this?

One might respond, sin is not a physical disease but a spiritual condition that requires forgiveness, not healing. If someone does wrong to me, it is the relationship that has been ruptured, not my spleen. I have it within my power to grant forgiveness, and if offered, the other person has the right to take it as a fact and act upon it. If the other person should continue to feel guilty, then we would say that this guilt has no objective basis and is merely "psychological guilt," which can be expiated through believing the words of forgiveness, not repeated confession.

This is partly the truth, but not the whole truth.

The splitting of the spiritual from our personal and social life is the root of the problem. I suggest that the theory of atonement which Anselm develops can easily contribute to this problem. According to the Bible, sin is not only a transgression of God's law which does require God's pardon, but it also has its effect upon our physical, psychological and social life. When the Christians at Corinth were so disorderly at the Lord's Table by excluding others and not "discerning the body," Paul warned them that "For this reason many of you are weak and ill, and some have died" (1 Cor. 11:30).

Those who have received the Spirit of Christ and forgiveness of sins in his name, Paul wrote, should no longer live under the "works of the flesh," as he put it. In naming these, Paul included: "fornication, impurity, licentiousness, idolatry, sorcery, enmities, strife, jealousy, anger, quarrels, dissensions, factions, envy, drunkenness, carousing, and things like these" (Gal. 5:19-21). In contrast, he listed the effects of living a life under the power of the Spirit as: "love, joy, peace, patience, kindness, generosity, faithfulness, gentleness, and self-control" (Gal. 5:22-23).

Clearly, the effects of forgiveness of sin through union with Christ go far beyond the removal of an objective guilt through divine pardon, though that is surely included. The whole truth of forgiveness includes the effects of sin as a continuing struggle in the Christian life which also must come under the sacrament of grace.

The church as the body of Christ is the sacrament of forgiveness and healing as the members share mutually in their common struggle and break the power of sin by mutual confession.

Dietrich Bonhoeffer introduced mutual confession of sins to his seminary students as a way of breaking through the self-deception of confessing only to God, as he put it. He asked why we should think it easier to confess our sins to God who is altogether holy than to a brother or sister who is a sinner like we are? He concluded that we think it is easier because we may only be confessing to ourselves and granting ourselves absolution, and that this is why there are so many relapses and lack of growth through confession.

While we may not have institutionalize mutual confession as a ritual in the way that Bonhoeffer attempted, we can see the truth of his insight. The power of sin is its secret life. The church becomes an accomplice in keeping this secret by affirming only those who appear to be righteous. All too often the last place that the Christian who is struggling with the addictive power of sin can share that struggle is with brothers and sisters in the church.

An alternative to the more traditional approach to the atonement can be found in the work of Thomas F. Torrance, who grounds the atonement in the threefold work of God as Father, Son and Holy Spirit. Torrance says that in the Old Testament God is never acted upon by priestly sacrifice offered by humans. It is always God himself who provides the sacrifice by which he draws near to humans and draws humans near to himself in the actualized liturgy of the life, death, resurrection and ascension of Jesus Christ.

Am I wrong in suggesting that when Christ returns he

will not be as pleased to see the empty cross as the universal symbol of Christian faith as he will be to find the "two or three gathered in his name" as the bearers of his own personal truth and the reality of the atonement (Matt. 18:20)? Did Jesus have to die on a cross? Well he did, but it was not the crosspieces of a tree nor the spilled blood which put an end to our sins. He didn't just bleed to death; he loved to death, and that love is alive and flowing freely through the Holy Spirit into our hearts to make us children of God. Let this be our song! Think about it!

7

Do I Have to Believe in Hell?

As a small boy, I worried more about eternal punishment in hell than I wondered about a blessed life in heaven. My first acquaintance with the concept of hell probably came from hearing sermons on the subject, but just as likely from idle conversations with my peers. Some of them, perhaps as a way of projecting their own fears, liked to scare others with imaginative scenarios of eternal torment in hell for committing a variety of sins, particularly those well known to small boys.

I am sure that these fears where reinforced by well meaning church school teachers who wanted to make sure that we understood the consequence of displeasing God as a way of molding obedient Christian life and faith.

My own particular fetish concerning eternal punishment involved an attempt to think about what it would be like to be in a terrible place where some kind of suffering continued forever. I would concentrate hard on the exact moment in which I could imagine that, at last, it would be over and then suddenly think, it will never be over! That moment had such a paralyzing effect on me that I immediately shut down my thinking process as the consequence was too terrible to even dwell on for a moment. From time to time, lying in bed at night, I would try the experiment again, as though drawn by an irresistible force to the exact moment when I came to the realization of what it meant for torment to go on without end. Each time I would draw back and repress the knowledge of this terrible thought as though I had never actually thought it. It was something like walking up to a precipice and standing precariously on the brink of an abyss about to lose one's balance and fall in. Eventually, of course, I seemed to outgrow the need for this "experiment" and thought very little again about hell until I went through the catechism class in our local Lutheran church as a young teenager where I rather glibly included "hell" in the catalogue of things which I confessed to "believe in."

Much later, even through my seminary study, I had little interest in the subject of hell, content to affirm it as a fixture which had its own place in the final eschatological scheme of things. It was only in assuming the role of pastor that I came upon the question again, this time from an anxious parishioner who challenged me one day with the question, "Pastor, do I have to believe in hell in order to belong to this church?" I actually do not remember the nature of my response, but in any event, the individual who asked the question did not leave!

If indeed, there is life after death, and retribution to follow for those who are found outside of God's saving grace, it may have some prenatal antecedent in human consciousness.

Halvard Solness, the master builder in Ibsen's play, admits that he is afraid to climb the scaffolding of a tower which he has built.

Hilda: Afraid of falling and killing yourself?
Solness: No, not that.
Hilda: What, then?
Solness: Afraid of retribution, Hilda.

Raised in a pious home, Solness worried that the structures which he built might be some kind of tower of Babel, a symbol of his rivalry with God. "I pretty well got the idea that He wasn't pleased with me."

Hamlet too worries about retribution after death, even as he ponders suicide as a welcome end to the slings and arrows of outrageous fortune:

But that dread of something after death,
The undiscover'd country from whose bourn

No traveler returns, puzzles the will,
And makes us rather bear those ills we have
Than fly to others that we know not of?
Thus conscience does make cowards of us all . . .
(Shakespeare: Hamlet, III. i)

Perhaps Hamlet has studied the Bible too. Death as a form of punishment for sin would seem to be sufficient. That at least would be an escape from the distress of life and the presence of God. One might well assume that the act of dying by itself would be sufficient payment for sin. After all, the Apostle Paul did say that the wages of sin is death (Rom. 6:23), and death is the punishment which falls upon the entire human race (Rom. 5:12-15). Why would God have need of raising people out of the grave only for the purpose of inflicting further, eternal torment? This is what causes a crisis of faith for many people. Do I have to believe that in order to be a Christian?

Scholars tell us that many ancient cultures also portray death as an evil which results from defilement of life, and even speak in lurid language about torment and judgment following death. This means that not only in the New Testament, but also in the literature of ancient Egypt, Iran, India, China and Japan, under the influence of Hinduism and Buddhism, references to punishment after death are to be found.

One thousand years before the time of Moses, inscriptions on the tombs of Egyptian kings reveal hopes of avoiding future punishment beyond death. Small boys in Egypt, too, go to sleep at night with visions of torment after death troubling them more than death itself.

It is a matter of some interest to note that the Old Testament, which is often regarded as depicting God's judgment in the most severe terms, has virtually nothing to say about punishment after death. After the fall (Genesis 3) death is not mentioned as a curse; rather, life itself comes under the burden of death as the ground is cursed and the dust from which humans were taken is left to swallow them again. It is surprising, then, to find in the New Testament the most specific and severe language regarding the state of torment following death for the wicked. Scholars have noted the developmental concept of rewards and punishment following death in the apocalyptic literature which emerged between the closing of the Old Testament canon and the ministry and teaching of Jesus. Jesus apparently used some of these concepts in depicting torment after death as experiencing the "anguish of flames" (Luke 16:24); being cast into "outer darkness" where some will "weep and knash their teeth" (Matthew 22:13); where "their worm does not die, and the fire is not quenched" (Mark 9:48). In the final apocalyptic vision of John, "the smoke of their torment goes up for ever and ever" (Revelation 14:11). It is God who is to be feared, not death, because he has the power to "cast into hell" (Luke 12:5).

The author of the book of Hebrews makes the solemn utterance, "It is appointed for mortals to die once, and after that the judgment." But this is immediately followed by the christological qualification, "so Christ, having been offered once to bear the sins of many, will appear a second time, not to deal with sin, but to save those who are eagerly waiting for him" (Hebrews 9: 27-28).

Whatever we make of the strong metaphors which the New Testament uses to speak of hell and its torments, we should remember that they are metaphors. For example, if hell is not only a place of "outer darkness" but at the same time a place where "the fire is not quenched," it is difficult to take both metaphors of darkness and fire literally. Two aspects of the biblical language regarding hell as the final destiny of the wicked are cause for reflection. First, the concept of hell as a "place" outside of God's reign and presence raises questions as to how something can exist as a "place" beyond God's sustaining Word and control. If God continues to maintain such a "place," then it cannot be outside of God's own will and power to sustain it as a reality independent of God's own being. To entertain such a concept would result in a dualism by which something (hell, for example) has real existence outside of God's own creative and sustaining power.

Again, if God is the source by which hell is maintained as a place or sphere of reality, then it cannot lie outside of God's control. One could say that God does not sustain hell as a place outside of his sphere of control, but this then would entail the concept that hell is maintained as a place by virtue of God's Word and will. Such a concept is rather foreign to a theological concept that the Word of God is the original source of all that is "good." not that which is essentially evil.

Secondly there is difficulty with regard to the concept of eternal torment in hell, which the apocalypse of John suggests by the words, "the smoke of their torment goes up *for ever and ever*" (14:11). The difficulty here is in assuming that "for ever and ever" might entail an endless continuation of what we call "time" as a specific chronological sequence of days, months, years, etc. If time as we know it is a structure of this created order and if, in the age to come, the heavens and earth will pass away, then time as we know it will no longer exist. To project a concept of time as self conscious awareness of minutes, hours, days, and years into an eternal order is at best an anthropomorphic metaphor and at worst, a misunderstanding of the difference between eternity and temporality.

Regarding the projection of a "time element" after death, Thomas Torrance says: "Looked at from the perspective of the new creation there is no gap between the death of the believer and the *parousia* of Christ, but looked at from the perspective of time that decays and crumbles away, there is a lapse of time between them."

From the perspective of our temporal order we can only project an interval of time between our death and resurrection of the body. The same would hold with regard to an existence in God's eternal life where time as we know it will hardly be counted, despite the familiar hymn, <u>Amazing Grace</u>: "When we've been there ten thousand years, bright shining as the sun, we've no less days to sing God's praise, than when we first begun."

I have no need to say that those who "believe in hell" and

in the concept of eternal punishment are wrong. Those who have no difficulty in thinking and believing in this way are attempting to be faithful to the biblical language which speaks of hell as a place and of torment as continuing for ever and ever.

Some, however, ask, "Do I have to believe in hell in order to be a Christian?" In attempting to answer this question, we need to probe a bit further into the theological meaning of the biblical language that speaks of hell as a place over and against heaven and eternal torment over and against eternal blessedness.

First of all, we should make a distinction between "eternal punishing" and "eternal punishment" (Matthew 25:46). The former entails an ongoing process involving continued time, whereas the latter suggests a once and for all action. Thus, some have interpreted the words of Jesus to mean that eternal punishment is equivalent to eternal destruction as contrasted to eternal life. The Apostle Paul, for example, warns that those who reject the gospel will suffer "the punishment of eternal destruction" (2 Thess. 1:9).

Setting aside the technical theological and exegetical issues, let me try a more imaginative approach, such as that with which I began in this chapter, reflecting upon my childhood attempt to imagine what hell would be like if it entailed endless days and years. Let us think of a state of blessedness, such as we are promised in being in the presence of God eternally, as somewhat like our occasional and temporary experiences. We have all had "times" in which we have been caught up in a state of euphoria, either alone or with others, in which we lose track of time. We may suddenly become aware of this and exclaim, "where has the time gone!" We become aware of a time interval only after losing consciousness of time due to the euphoric state. In this way, one might conceive of a state of eternal blessedness as existence within the very being and presence of God as not dependent upon time itself. Thus, eternal blessedness in God's presence would be heaven, without time.

What then would be the opposite of this? That is to say, what would banishment from God's presence be like (eternal punishment) without conscious time involved? We cannot suddenly introduce a time element into eternal punishment when we have no time element in eternal blessedness. Some might protest at this "thought experiment" and say that they cannot conceive of heaven without the self conscious passing of time. I concede that, as we find it virtually incomprehensible to conceive of existence without time.

But God's existence is both a mystery to us and a revelation. As a matter of revelation, God's existence is eternal love, and as a mystery, we can neither comprehend the depth of that love nor the extent of it.

If all of our "thinking" of the things that belong to God must conform to God's self revelation and, if Christ is the revelation of both God's inner being of love and God's eternal purpose of love, then we are not permitted to "think outside of Jesus Christ" in our theological reflection. This is an important theme in the theological methodology of Thomas Torrance when he said, "Jesus not only determined for us in himself the true mode of religious and theological questioning but constituted himself as the very centre of reference for our questions about God."

In following out this line of thought we may say that in becoming human, God not only assumed death as belonging to humanity as a consequence of sin, but hell as well. If Jesus "descended into hell," as the Apostle's Creed rightly states, then he was not only raised from the grave in the resurrection; he was raised from hell! Hell is an extension of humanity, not something beyond what is human.

The question as to the reality of hell is now one aspect of our Christology. If there was a hell for Jesus, there is a hell. The question of the population of hell is not for us to say. We know that God has been to hell, if Jesus indeed descended into hell. We know that Jesus was raised from hell. We know that hell is within the grasp of God, not beyond his power, if Jesus has been raised from hell.

All questions regarding the ultimate destiny of human persons must be asked "through Jesus Christ," as Thomas Torrance once said. We are not permitted to attribute to God motives and intentions beyond what are revealed to us through Christ. Christ is the "alpha and omega," the beginning and the end of our knowledge of God (Rev. 1:8; 21:6).

We can be assured, therefore, that hell has no threat to those who are raised with Christ, as Paul uses the phrase (Col. 3:1; Eph. 2:6). The decisive point with regard to the eternal destiny of humans is not an abstract mathematical number determined by limiting Christ's death only for some, nor by including every human in Christ's death. When Christ died, all died even as when Adam sinned all sinned, argues Paul (Rom. 5). The decisive point is in the power of the resurrection, and the reality of spiritual rebirth into the life of Christ through the Holy Spirit. All have died with Christ, but not all have been raised with Christ.

The point is, in becoming human through Jesus Christ, God sent his Son as far from heaven as necessary in order to provide salvation and reconciliation for humans. In descending into hell, Jesus did not have to take a step beyond what he took in becoming human; he took a step into the abyss which lies within the nature and possibility of every human created in God's image.

How far is hell from heaven? No further than the span between Jesus and the Father. Jesus "emptied himself" of all self-determination in order to follow the fate of his fellow humans into the deepest crevice of human estrangement. He was fully human, fully prepared to die, fully prepared to descend into hell.

How far was Jesus sent into the world? Farther than any human has ever gone and come back. He assumed the form of humanity, under sentence of death, and took it straight to hell where the Father found him and brought him back to life and glory.

Do I have to believe in hell?

It depends upon what we mean by "believe in." To believe

in something is to affirm the reality of that which God has created and which exists through God's power and Word. God originally said, "Let there be light" (Genesis 1:3). God did not say, "let there be darkness." Darkness did not exist prior to light. Nothing existed prior to the creative Word of God. When God created light, darkness suddenly emerged as the shadow side of light. When God said, "Let [this or that] be," we know that nonbeing lies on the other side of being. We cannot believe in that which does not exist as a result of the creative Word of God. We cannot believe in that which God does not affirm as the good. We must deal with the phenomenological reality of the non-good, as we deal with disease, demons and death. But we are not to *believe* in such phenomena, but rather to set the Word and power of God over and against that which opposes the good and God. Thus, Karl Barth says: "We cannot believe in the devil and demons as we believe in angels when we believe in God. We have a positive relationship to that in which we believe. But there is no positive relationship to the devil and demons. We cannot ignore them. We must know about them, but only as the limit of that to which a positive relationship is possible and legitimate and obligatory."

I believe that Jesus Christ descended into hell following his death on the cross and there suffered the "eternal punishment," including all of the torment of which the Bible speaks. Nothing should be taken away from the reality of the language used in the New Testament concerning hell and eternal punishment as a consequence of total estrangement from God. But, at the same time, nothing should be "left outside" of the punishment which Christ assumed and endured on behalf of human beings.

I believe that Christ was not only raised from the grave but also raised from hell. This belief is grounded in the positive relationship which is assured to us by the Spirit of Christ which dwells in us, by which we are "rescued from the power of darkness and transferred into the kingdom of his beloved Son..." (Col. 1:13). I believe that in the final judgment, Christ himself will determine the eternal destiny of all humans.

Now, when I meditate on eternal life I do so from the inside out, not as a questioning bystander, but through the witness of the Holy Spirit who gives a gracious answer before I have time to come to the end of my questioning.

There was no vision of Christ in the dark and threatening picture of eternal punishment that I, as a small boy, carried to my bed. There are some who will be sure that it was this threat of unending torment which drove that small boy later to accept the answer which Christ provides. But they will be wrong, for Christ came on his own terms, from his own death and resurrection, bringing healing and peace. Think about it!

8

Should I Pray for a Miracle

The woman sitting in my office was distraught and angry. As she talked, I began to feel that she had good reason to be so upset. Her adolescent daughter had a history of drug related problems, had stolen her mother's credit card, had withdrawn a large sum from the bank, and had left home to live with two other teenagers with a man twice their age.

"I am heart-sick over this," she told me, "and angry. Angry not only at her for what she has done to me but angry at God for not protecting her." I encouraged her to talk about her feelings toward God. "What has God done or failed to do in protecting your daughter?"

"This is my only child. My husband and I almost gave up trying to have children. I read in the Bible where Hannah, who was without a child, prayed to the Lord and she received a child in answer to her prayer. His name was Samuel. I prayed that God would enable me to conceive, and that if I did I would give this child to God in the same way that Hannah did with her son, Samuel. When my daughter was born I knew that she was an answer to prayer; I named her Samantha."

I waited.

"I kept praying for her, especially when she began to get in trouble. I wonder now if it makes any difference to pray. I wonder if there really is a God, and if there is, why he doesn't put a shield of protection around those who belong to him. I hear stories of other people praying for miracles and they happen! Don't I have a right to expect a miracle too when I pray?"

In no area of the Christian life is there more uncertainty,

confusion and even a sense of failure than in our life of prayer. Many of us were taught as children to pray. Later, prayer was urged upon us as a source of spiritual renewal and blessing as well as a way to secure God's answers for our physical as well as spiritual needs. We were reminded of the answers to prayer achieved by many of God's saints as a means of challenging us to a deeper and more sustained prayer life. And yet, we so seldom realize answers for our prayers.

Our children for whom we pray are not always healed of disease and spared the pain of grievous loss. Friends for whom we intercede with fervent prayer still suffer catastrophic illness and lingering, painful deaths. Yes, there are the occasional almost miraculous exceptions to which we cling with nervous faith and of which we speak in a too-shrill voice, as if to fill the void of heaven's silence too long endured. But earnestly inquire of us concerning our confidence in prayer to feed the hungry, heal the sick, salvage broken marriages, produce saving faith in loved ones, and we confess more failure than success.

In a discussion about prayer with my students I suggested that we really do not become strong in faith until we are able to live with unanswered prayer. The fact is, I went on to say, very few of our prayers are answered in the way that we expect. The response was exactly what I expected. "Then why pray at all," one retorted. Another said, "Unanswered prayer is a sign of weak faith. If you had sufficient faith, as Jesus said, your prayers would be answered." "All prayers are answered," offered one student; "sometimes the answer is no!" I was not convinced. Rather than to take "no for an answer." I held to my conviction that most prayers are simply not answered.

Others told stories of miracles performed in answer to prayer, which primarily had to do with physical healing or the solving of a severe financial problem through an unexpected gift. As the anecdotes were recited it appeared that physical health and money were most often cited as examples of miraculous intervention in answer to prayer.

I thought of the woman who had prayed, like Hannah of old, who thought of her child as an answer to prayer, and in prayer, had given her to God, only to watch her life fall into ruin. What seemed an answer to prayer turned out to be a disaster, as far as the mother was concerned.

"Should I now pray for a miracle that Samantha be healed of her emotional, moral and spiritual sickness?"

I responded by saying, "yes, but I think that in the meantime we should think about some kind of intervention which may involve placing her under supervised treatment and care."

I told her about the case of a woman, now in her middle 50s who had suffered a paralyzing accident when she was 18, which left her paraplegic and confined to a wheelchair. She went on to earn a Ph. D. in clinical psychology and now works in a rehabilitation center for persons recovering from incapacitating injuries. A young man was admitted who had suffered a spinal cord injury and was in a wheel chair, unable to walk. Being a devout Christian, he insisted that God was going to heal him and that he would get up and walk out of the place as people in his church were praying for him.

Not wishing to destroy his faith which appeared to be the only coping mechanism he had with which to face the devastating loss of bodily function, she asked: "When do you think the miracle will come? Will it probably come tomorrow, or maybe next week?" He responded by saying, "I don't know, but God knows and when he answers our prayers I will be healed."

"That is good," she said. "Now let us see what we can do about learning how to use your fingers to hold a knife and fork so that you can feed yourself, until the miracle comes." With this, he consented to work on his physical therapy routine which he had been resisting based on his expectation of a miracle.

As this woman told the story to my class, sitting in her own wheel chair, she as much as said, "This is what I have accomplished waiting for the miracle to come." She too had been the object of intense prayer for healing at the time of her injury, but had long since given up her faith that God performed miracles. At the same time, as a good therapist, she was wise and supporting in not destroying the faith of the young man while, at the same time, helping him to prepare for a life where there would be no answer to prayer for miracles.

I tend to be a realist when it comes to prayer, though some may think of it as cynicism. Let me say as clearly as I can, I do believe that miracles occur and that there are miraculous answers to prayer. In the forty some years of my own ministry, I must say that I have never witnessed what I call a "flat out" miraculous healing, though I have witnessed many people for whom we have prayed gradually recover from illness and sickness. I do not doubt the accounts of miraculous healing that are told, though these appear to be so infrequent, despite intense and prevailing prayer, that there seems little statistical difference in the general health and survival rate between people who pray and the general population. Some are quick to remind me, however, that the purpose of a miracle may be that God is glorified and his power over sickness and death is displayed so that we can honor him. I have found that those who fail to receive a miracle in answer to prayer are often confused and angry to hear that God answers some prayers and not others.

I am well aware that miraculous healing in answer to prayer is part of a widespread movement, with a variety of assumptions and emphases. The so-called "faith healing" movement may be the most predominant. The logic of what has been called the "faith formula," is based on a three-fold premise: first, God wills health (bodily, spiritually, emotionally) for every Christian in this present age; second, God has pledged himself to heal every person from every sickness based on the atoning work of Christ on the cross; third, through faith and prayer one can, and should, claim this healing.

For example, the English theologian and pastor John Baker argues that God has promised complete healing in this life-time for those who have the faith to claim it. "It is our conviction that healing at every level of the person (including the physical) is part of God's provision of salvation during the New Testament age of grace." The possibilities for healing, according to Baker, "are only limited by what we can believe the Lord for." He does allow for the fact that some who pray in faith are not healed, but then attributes this to lack of faith on the part of the church where an "unbelieving" spiritual environment may hinder the Lord's work of healing. T. J. McCrossan makes even a stronger case, suggesting that when one prays for healing one should never say to God, "If it is your will. . . no one can possibly pray the prayer of faith which saves the sick (James 5:15) and put in the proviso 'if it be thy will.'"

The premise underlying these attempts to place the responsibility for securing a miraculous healing in answer to prayer upon our faith is that through the death of Jesus on the cross, God has not only provided immediate forgiveness of sins based on our faith, but has also provided for immediate physical healing based on the same faith. Thus, it is claimed, "healing is in the atonement."

New Testament scholar Gordon Fee refutes this claim by arguing that the atoning death of Jesus on the cross had only to do with assurance of forgiveness of sins through faith and not with complete bodily healing in this life time. The healing aspect of Christ's death and resurrection, Fee suggests, is eschatological. All evils, including suffering, sickness, congenital deformities, and Satanic resistance are part of the consequences of the Fall. All are included in the promise of eschatological victory. Jesus came announcing the reality of the Kingdom of God as the eschatological reality and power of God which is the revelation (apocalypse) of God's power and healing presence. Through his death and resurrection, the powers and evils of this age were brought under divine judgment, and total victory and healing is accomplished. The gift of the Holy Spirit is the eschatological inauguration of the "new age" and the seal and promise of salvation, with healing ultimately assured through the resurrection of the dead.

The so-called "faith passages" in the New Testament (Matt. 11:24; 17:20; Luke 17:6; Mark 9:23; James 1:6) are commonly misconstrued says Fee. "The real issue, therefore, when it comes to these texts, is not how 'to get them to work for us,' but how we are to understand them in the light of the full biblical revelation. How do they relate to the reality of God's sovereignty and His overall purposes for mankind?" Has God really "covenanted" (promised) that physical healing would be granted on the same basis as forgiveness of sins simply through faith? My colleague Colin Brown thinks not. "If God heals, it is an uncovenanted mercy. But when he forgives, it is a covenanted mercy." Brown suggests that when God does intervene with a miraculous healing, it is simply due to God's sovereign freedom and power. The church is given authority to announce forgiveness of sins in this present age, says Brown, but it has no parallel authority to heal.

My response is to say that both forgiveness of sins and perfect healing of all disease and illness are eschatological realities based on the resurrection of Jesus from the dead. It is not on the cross that the consequence of sin was overcome, but through resurrection. The Apostle Paul wrote: "If Christ has not been raised, your faith is futile and you are still in your sins" (1 Cor. 15:17). Jesus corrected his disciples when they suggested that there is a cause and effect relation between sin and sickness. "Who sinned, this man or his parents that he was born blind? (John 9:2). "Neither," responded Jesus. In so doing he broke this connection which continues to this day to torment persons. A specific illness, birth defect, or injury is not to be construed as the result of some specific sin. The fact that we receive both forgiveness of sin and healing of disease through Christ's death and resurrection does not mean that a specific sin causes a specific disease or disability.

In this context Paul is arguing for the reality of the resurrection of Jesus as a basis by which we can be assured of our own resurrection. At the same time, he makes clear that apart from the resurrected life of Jesus Christ, the consequence of sin is not removed, even by the death of Jesus on the cross. In retrospect, after the resurrection of Jesus, one can indeed say, "Christ died for our sins" (1 Cor. 15:3). But the pronouncement of forgiveness of sins is also tied to our own resurrection so that if it should be that I am not ultimately raised from the dead, my sins will not in fact have been forgiven. But through the Spirit of the resurrected Christ in me I have present assurance of my future resurrection (forgiveness) and also of complete healing.

I would then argue that healing is in the atonement along with forgiveness of sins, but that both are eschatological realities of which we have present assurance through the Spirit of Christ. However, the present assurance of forgiveness of sins should not be taken to be ambiguous or uncertain, even though miraculous healing of physical illness may be. For it is the witness of the Holy Spirit in our hearts that gives us this present assurance (Rom. 8:9-11; 26-27).

What then do we say about the occurrence in our present time of a miraculous healing? First, all such healings are provisional and temporary, in that the person healed will eventually suffer death. No miracle of healing delivers a person from the inevitability of death. Even Lazarus, who was raised from the dead (John 11), did not experience the kind of resurrection that Jesus later experienced, but only a resuscitation, having to die again at some later point. Second, the miracle of healing under these conditions can best be understood as an eschatological sign in the present age pointing to the future resurrection.

This leads me finally to suggest that a physical healing which is recognized as miraculous, is a kind of sacrament, by which the ultimate reality of resurrection and therefore forgiveness of sins is assured to the church and to the one who experiences the healing. This is not to suggest that we add a third sacrament to the Eucharist and Baptism. These two sacraments are clearly instituted by Christ and are available to all Christians, whereas the miracle of physical healing is apparently not. We can, however, think of a miracle in a sacramental way, without making it into a sacrament. By this is meant that the eschatological reality of the resurrection as the basis for hope is represented in the miracle of healing as a communication of this hope to all Christians, not merely to those who are healed.

Viewing the miracle of physical healing of a person as a kind of sacrament, or sign of the resurrection, delivers the person who is healed from the implied consequence of the healing as some kind of freedom from sickness and disease as a condition of life. The person who is healed may well subsequently die of either a return of the same disease, or another disease, without the effect and meaning of the healing in any way diminished. The effect of the healing is to strengthen faith in the reality of the resurrection and the forgiveness of sins, not to make faith dependent upon the effect of the healing itself.

In the same way, the miracle of physical healing of a person considered as an eschatological sign of the resurrection delivers the church from the temptation to set up physical healing as a special sign of God's grace for those who have sufficient faith. The church is thus delivered from the tendency to make out of physical healing a manipulation of faith and a pragmatic method by which the growth of the church can be assured. That which has the character of a sacrament is an eschatological event and can never be subject to control or manipulation.

How then should we pray for a miracle if most prayers are not answered and miracles are few and far between?

God is like a parent, and we have every reason to think in this way. Jesus taught us to pray to "our father in heaven," and the Apostle Paul urged us to think of receiving the Spirit of adoption into God's family whereby we cry, "Abba! Father!" (Rom. 8:15). If God is like a parent, then we must place prayer into that relational context rather than view prayer as "pulling a lever" and expecting the "treat to drop."

When children beg for something from a parent, it is like a petition or prayer for something which they earnestly need or think they need. At least they have their heart set on something which only the parent can provide. Most such begging (praying) goes unanswered if not unheeded. Suddenly, the parent will, for no apparent reason, relent and give in to the request. Now the child does not ordinarily say, "I must have asked in just the right way this time, and if I learn how to ask in this way I will always get an answer." No, the child simply accepts the fact that this is how it is with parents. The child does not suffer loss of confidence and trust in the parent through an extended time of unanswered begging (prayer). Nor does the child blame him or herself when the request goes unanswered. Though it must also be said that children can become quite devious with respect to manipulating their parents through insistent begging. Something of the same might be said of how many Christians use prayer in relation to their heavenly father!

We are not amazed that the prayers of Jesus were heard and answered by the Father on each occasion when he prayed for others. Yet we have come to expect that our own prayers often seem to go unanswered, or perhaps unheard. We know that we do not pray as we ought, and that our prayers so often are desperate and devoid of the inner certainty which comes from an intimate communion with God, our heavenly Father.

In his high priestly prayer, Jesus not only prays for his disciples, "whom you gave me," but also for all who would come to believe in the Father through Jesus. "I ask not only on behalf of these, but also on behalf of those who will believe in me through their word, that they may all be one. As you, Father, are in me and I am in you, may they also be in us, so that the world may believe that you have sent me" (John 17:20-21). The disciples are but the inner core of a circle whose circumference is as extensive as all of humanity.

But we are surprised when we see that the prayer of Jesus when he chose the twelve to follow him resulted in the calling of Judas, his own betrayer (Luke 6). And we are left to question the effectiveness of Jesus' prayer when Judas was allowed at the end to follow through with his evil act. We would expect Jesus, after a night of prayer, to have discovered what God already knew—Judas would be the betrayer. In the same way, when we pray we often expect to gain an advantage in determining ahead of time the will of God so that we do not fail in some venture, or go in the wrong direction and have to "back-track" in order to get back into the will of God.

This reveals to us how our life of prayer is often based on our misunderstanding of love and grace. When we view God's grace as conditional upon our perfection and success in living by his commandments, we will tend to use prayer as a way of securing God's promises by meeting the right conditions. In this view of God, a failure to produce a result through prayer throws us back upon our own lack of faith or, even worse, some spiritual defect which lies unconfessed and which sabotages God's work.

On the other hand, if we view God's providence and foreknowledge as some kind of "pre-written history," then we will use prayer to gain access to that secret knowledge of God—to take a peek at the answers in the back of the book, if you please!

What we discover, instead, is that the will of God is grounded in his promise as to the outcome of our lives, not in a detailed plan which remains hidden in the mind of God. Prayer is thus access to the divine promise revealed through the inner relation which the Son shares with the Father rather than an attempt to avoid the risk of failure. Through his life of prayer with the Father, Jesus could love unconditionally and freely the unknown elements in his disciples as well as the known qualities. In this way, even the actions of Judas as betrayer are included within the divine promise and purpose for Jesus. Prayer, for Jesus, was not for the purpose of excluding the sinful actions of others, but for including all persons, despite their failures, in his own life with the Father as the basis for redemption of sinners.

Yes, we should pray for a miracle, but then invest our faith in God rather than in prayer. Do I believe in prayer? No. I believe in God, and pray to God and look to God for the faith to live with unanswered prayer.

What can we do until the miracle comes? Have faith and exercise our fingers in order to learn to feed ourselves. Think about it!

9

Does God Allow Evil in Order to Produce Good?

Her story was tragic and deeply disturbing. Six months prior to coming to me for pastoral guidance, her seven year old daughter had died of a brain aneurysm on a Sunday evening while she and her husband were attending a service in their church. The child had been left home with a babysitter and they were summoned out of the service by paramedics who responded to the call for help.

Tragic as this sudden death was and her grief over the loss of their only child, what happened next was disturbing and the cause of her outrage directed against God. The funeral service for the girl was held in the church with the pastor officiating. During the service, in an attempt to bring some meaning and comfort to the parents, he suggested that God wanted to bring spiritual renewal to the members of the church and had selected one of their most prominent families and had taken their daughter home to be with the Lord, where she was far better off than to live in this world. God's purpose in doing this, the Pastor went on to say, was to cause the members of the church to reflect upon the brevity of life and to call them to repentance and renewed commitment to the Lord. He then gave an invitation for those who wished to acknowledge their new commitment to Christ to come forward for a prayer of dedication. Following the service she never again went back to the church.

As the woman told me this story, her face flushed with anger and she said, "I could never worship a God who would do that!" She went on to express her anger at God for killing her child, even expressing feelings of unbelief in God's existence. I remained silent, except to agree with her that a God who would do such a thing in order to coerce others into a response of deeper commitment was not the God that I could worship. I moved my chair alongside hers and took her side against God. After many minutes during which she poured out her anger at God, she paused and, taking a deep breath, said, "I really don't believe that God killed my child. But what other reason could there be for her death? Isn't God in control of everything that happens? If he loved her in the way that we do, why could he not have intervened and saved her?"

At the time, I was only a year or two out of seminary, and no discussion in my theology classes had ever dealt with this question, other than to affirm the importance of upholding the attributes of both God's sovereignty and goodness. Now, faced with this question, in the face of this woman's grief and suffering, I found the traditional arguments for God's goodness and sovereignty quite inadequate.

To my surprise, she did not really demand an answer to her question. She only wanted the permission to ask it. As I directed her to consider the tears of Jesus at the tomb of his friend Lazarus as the very tears and grief of God, she left feeling closer to God than when she came. But it was a different God than the one she carried into the room on the crest of her anguish and anger.

Years later, I discovered the book by Rabbi Harold Kushner, <u>When Bad Things Happen to Good People</u>. His son died at the age of fourteen, following extended illness due to progeria, the rapid aging disease. Failing to reconcile this tragedy with the theological concepts of God's power and love with which he had been trained, he wrote the book in which he raised the question as to whether God could be both all powerful and good. "I believe in God," he wrote,

> But I do not believe the same things about Him that I did years ago, when I was growing up or when I was a theological student. I recognize His limitations. He is limited in what He can do by laws of nature and by the evolution of human nature and moral freedom. I no longer hold God responsible for illnesses, accidents, and natural

disasters, because I realize that I gain little and I lose so much when I blame God for those things. I can worship a God who hates suffering but cannot eliminate it, more easily than I can worship a God who chooses to make children suffer and die, for whatever exalted reason.

When I ask my students to read this book and respond to Kushner, a great deal of anxiety is produced. Most feel sympathetic toward the Rabbi but rush to defend God's sovereignty. Some suggest that because Kushner is not a Christian and does not understand that God destroyed the power of sickness and death through Jesus Christ, he is unable to retain a concept of God's sovereignty. Invariably, they end by some kind of appeal to God's permissive will during the interim time, where suffering continues due to sin, but for which there will be compensation in the end. I often urge them never to offer this bit of wisdom to someone who is actually suffering! Whatever our concept of suffering and the reality of evil, we do well to remember that for the one who suffers, it will always be perceived as evil and not as good.

To tell a woman that the death of her young child was God's plan to develop in her a deeper spiritual life and a stronger character will likely provoke the response, "I would rather have my child and remain weaker in character, given the choice." Some who have gone through the cycle of self development, experiencing grief and loss and who finally survive, may well testify to a faith and hope that is stronger by virtue of having stood the test. But only those who have suffered such grief have the right to make such a statement.

Can we believe in a God who permits evil that good may come?

Ivan Karamozov, a character in one of Dostoyevsky's novels, does not think so. Ivan challenges the theology of his brother Alyosha, a novice in residence to become a monk. Ivan recounts incidents of the torture of children, and one case of a general who set his dogs on a boy chewing the child to bits before the eyes of his mother. When Aloysha protests and suggests that this horrible crime can only be explained by submitting to the inscrutable will and purpose of God,

Ivan responds with outrage bordering on blasphemy in his brother's eyes. "Listen! If all must suffer to pay for the eternal harmony, what have children to do with it, tell me, please? It's beyond all comprehension why they should suffer, and why they should pay for the harmony. Why should they, too, furnish material to enrich the soil for the harmony of the future? I understand solidarity in sin among men. I understand solidarity in retribution, too; but there can be no such solidarity with children."

Sensing the protest mounting in Aloysha, Ivan continues: " Oh, Aloysha, I am not blaspheming! I understand, of course, what an upheaval of the universe it will be, when everything in heaven and earth blends in one hymn of praise and everything that lives and has lived cries aloud: 'Thou art just, O Lord, for Thy ways are revealed.' When the mother embraces the fiend who threw her child to the dogs, and all three cry aloud with tears, 'Thou art just, O Lord!' then, of course, the crown of knowledge will be reached and all will be made clear. But what pulls me up here is that I can't accept that harmony."

What Ivan cannot accept is the theological answer to the problem of evil that God will finally reconcile all things to himself and reveal a pattern of perfect justice that will vindicate him and produce a final harmony. Not even retribution against the offender will satisfy the injustice that this horrible evil was permitted. No forgiveness and no atonement can wipe away the **fact** that a grievous wrong was done. "I don't want harmony," Ivan cries out, "From love for humanity I don't want it. I would rather be left with the unavenged suffering. I would rather remain with my unavenged suffering and unsatisfied indignation, *even if I were wrong*. Besides, too high a price is asked for harmony; it's beyond our means to pay so much to enter on it. And so I hasten to give back my entrance ticket, and if I am an honest man I am bound to give it back as soon as possible. And that I am doing. It's not God that I don't accept, Alyosha, only I must respectfully return Him the ticket."

With less eloquence, but with equal passion, the woman who had lost her child was close to "giving back her ticket," if it meant being asked to believe that God had a reason and the power to weave the death of her child into some eternal harmony of peace and joy. While I had not found in my earlier theological training a response to her question, I had read Dostoyevsky and understood well the complaint of Ivan against a too simplistic explanation for the evil which afflicts the human condition.

I had also read the complaint of the Old Testament prophet Habakkuk who was prepared to call God to account for the injustice he saw all around. The question raised by Habakkuk was the opposite of the one by Kushner. "Why do good things happen to bad people," Habakkuk wanted to know. "Your eyes are too pure to behold evil, and you cannot look on wrongdoing; why do you look on the treacherous, and are silent when the wicked swallow those more righteous than they?" (Habakkuk 1:13). One looks in vain for a philosophical answer to his challenge. God's response is succinct and apparently sufficient, "the righteous live by their faith" (2:4). God accepts the charge that there is injustice in the world and does not defend himself, but only says, in effect, "who else is there to trust but the One who created and upholds all things and who loves you?"

God does not duck and dodge the reality of evil, attributing it to human sin and blaming it on the Devil. God is the author of the drama in which pain and pleasure, suffering and joy, good and evil are part of the plot. Faith means that we as human participants in that drama know that there is an author and that the drama is being constructed even as we live it out. The righteous do not live by their righteousness, God reminded Habakkuk, but by faith. God takes full responsibility. This, at least, is a start.

The theological question with regard to suffering is: What does it mean to say that God takes responsibility for evil and that we can have faith in him to do this? The biblical tradition has no view of evil as a problem outside of the concept of God's providence. God's providence is expressed through his partnership with human persons in suffering, which is the divine power to be present as our advocate in the context of suffering and for the purpose of redeeming those who suffer. The providence of God is bound to his promise. This promise is a miracle and mystery of divine love. Suffering and injustice can produce a crisis of faith, leading us directly to God as the one who must ultimately take responsibility. In his taking responsibility through participation in the dilemma of evil, God provides redemption from evil, not simply a solution to it as a problem.

This is why, for example, the dramatic story of Job is told in such a way that the Devil is permitted to inflict Job with catastrophic losses, and yet is limited by God as to the destruction of Job himself. God is the author of the drama of life, and he can allow the characters he has placed in the story to run the course of their role and live out the character assigned to each. At the same time, God has the 'story under control,' so to speak. And this, in the end, is the message of the book of Job.

We are troubled by the fact that the Devil and God seem to conspire against Job, and that God would allow such evil to exist. We want a different story, where we can sort out the good and the bad from the beginning and ensure that we are always on the good side! But we are not the author. For the Hebrew people, it was sufficient to know that God was not only one who could enter into the story at will, but who also had the story under control. They knew that the source of salvation was not in a perfect world, but in God who kept the story under control and who could be trusted to preserve their lives in the end. Ultimately, their trust in God was grounded in his love and his covenant promise. They understood God's providence to be aligned with his covenant promise, not with nature. Attempts to read God's purpose out of the events which occur in the natural world always leads to futility or fatalism.

The traditional concept of God's sovereignty viewed God

as controlling (causing) every detail and event in human history. The alternative to this was held to be chaos and confusion, leaving humans subject to the capricious winds of fate and fortune. Even the ancients looked to the stars, if not the entrails of animals, for an explanation and cause of what appeared to be random events. To live in a world without a supervening order and cause was more than the human spirit could bear. Where religion took away freedom, it gave back certainty, which, in the end, made fatalism more comforting than faith.

That God is in control, is certain, at least as one reads the Scriptures. But being "in control" does not mean "controlling every event," I tell my students. The root metaphor of God's relation to the world is not power, as in being Creator, but love, as in being parent. When God's power is grounded in God as Creator, it becomes mechanical and merciless.

Process theologians John Cobb and David Ray Griffen contrast these two kinds of power. "The problem of God's relation to evil is usually couched in terms of the first image of power. People want to know, therefore, why God does not snatch a child out of the way of a backing car, stop a bullet that is about to kill an innocent person (or stop the finger that was about to pull the trigger), or prevent the operation of the Nazi death camps. Superman is pictured as doing things like that. If God is even more powerful than Superman, why does God stand idly by? We would despise Superman if he did so."

This the kind of power which is viewed as a quantitative magnification of the kind of power which we use when we want to force something to conform to our will or to produce something by making a product. Cobb and Griffen argue that God uses a different kind of power, based on God's creative love. "We should not think of God as a super-Superman, out-coercing the coercive forces of the world. Rather, God has the evocative, inspiring, transforming power needed by the all-pervasive, loving, creator of the universe."

God's power is a different kind of power, not a lesser power, as Kushner suggested. We are not forced to choose between God's power and God's love, but rather to find in God's love the power to grant freedom to the created order while at the same time, exercise ultimate control over it.

If we conceive of God's control more like that of a parent who loves rather than a creator who coerces, we can find a helpful analogy in the way that parents often relate to their children. For example, parents may take their children in a car with the purpose of an outing at a recreation park. As they depart everything is going on schedule until some unforeseen events begin to transpire, such as a highway construction project which forces a detour or a flat tire on the car which requires the assistance of a tow truck. These events are unpredicted and purely random, out of control of the parents in the sense that they could have either predicted or prevented them. The children do not blame the parents for these happenings, but are only concerned that they really do arrive at their destination. The parents assure the children that they are "in control" of the situation even though changes will occur which will affect their arrival time, etc.

The point of this analogy is that in somewhat the same way we can say that God is in control of the world and of our lives, but does not control, or cause, every event to take place. This allows for both the freedom to initiate and complete actions within the limitations of our finite and temporal existence, but also ensures that in God's providence, his purpose for our lives will be completed.

More recently, theologians have argued this position under the concept of "open theism," where God not only acts so as to cause certain events to take place, but God also reacts to things as they take place. There is then, in this view, an allowance for a certain degree of randomness in the way in which things occur in this world without surrendering overall control with regard to the final outcome.

The overall theme of Scripture gives us an understanding of God as acting and reacting as a contemporary presence in our lives. I would begin with a more Christological analysis of God's relation to the world where God's power is grounded in God's love for the world expressed through the incarnation, death and resurrection of Jesus.

Does God permit suffering and allow evil to impact our lives in order to produce some good? The answer is no. The fact that "all things work together for good for those who love God" (Romans 8:28), cannot mean that God uses evil things to bring about good. Rather, in spite of evil, God works through all things to bring about good as the outcome of our faith and trust in him.

The death of this woman's child was not predetermined by God, was not known by God "in advance," and was not caused by God. When we undertake to love so as to bring forth life, such as the birth of a child, we participate in creating some of the very pain and sorrow which is inevitable for love to exist in this world. In bringing our three daughters into the world through our love, we ensured that there would someday be three graves at the end, many tears along the way, and even some inexplicable sufferings for them and for us. To embrace possibility with love is to embrace the tragic as well as the triumphant. Love does not dwell on this, but in the end, love knows how to accept it. God is love. Think about it.

10

When Does Human Life Begin, and End?

A nationally known insurance company advertises its product by showing a person holding a miniature house in outstretched hands accompanied by the slogan, "You're in good hands with . . .(fill in the name!)." The debate over the use of artificially inseminated human embryos to produce stem cells for scientific research presents a parallel, if not a more sinister, picture. On the one hand, some of the scientists involved argue for the necessity of this research using stem cells harvested from human embryos as a way of finding cures for the devastating diseases which debilitate and destroy adult human life. On the other hand, some of the politicians responsible for legislating the moral standards which protect human life under the constitution argue against this procedure on the grounds that it violates the most vulnerable form of human life.

Each hand has its duly constituted ethical authorities to argue its case. The scientists rely on the scholarly research and writing in the field of bioethics for their moral guidance. The politicians have their own stable of specialists in the field of social ethics to strengthen their hand.

Each hand offers its own slogan as a soundbite on the evening news. The one hand says, "Human life does not begin in a refrigerator but in a womb." The other hand responds, "These children (embryos) should be adopted and given a chance to grow up like other children."

Is human life in good hands? Think about it!

Jesus said, when it comes to making an offering to God, "when you give alms, do not let your left hand know what your right hand is doing" (Matthew 6:3). In the current debate over the inception of human life, one wonders whether each hand knows what the other hand is doing. Is this good?

One wonders how the pastors on the front line of ministry to their congregations preach on this subject. What texts do they find from the Bible to inform their preaching? And if they do preach so as to communicate an authoritative word from God, do they know what they are doing?

And what if the pastors turn back to their former seminary faculty professors for wisdom on the subject? Will they find mostly silence, or at best, a referral to the ethics department where the latest thinking from the field of bioethics and social ethics dominate the curriculum?

I am reminded of a comic strip called Peanuts, written by the late Charles Schulz, where Linus presented a drawing he had made to Lucy for her response. "This person doesn't have hands," she replied scornfully. "You have drawn him with his hands behind his back. This is because you yourself are immature and lacking in confidence." "No replied Linus, "It is because I myself can't draw hands."

I am beginning to wonder whether or not theologians can "draw hands;" or, metaphor apart, have confidence enough in their knowledge of what God intended in creating human life to offer wisdom with respect to what we are doing when we take human life literally, in hand.

Well, as the saying goes, fools rush in where angels fear to tread!

When it comes to the beginning and ending of life, we are always standing in the middle. I was not present at the beginning of my life, and will hardly be in a position to make serious observations at the end. With regard to the human race itself, we seem to have awakened already involved in the process.

In her book, *An American Childhood*, Annie Dillard wrote of her own awakening to self consciousness: "Children ten years old wake up and find themselves here, discover themselves to have been here all along; is this sad? They wake like sleepwalkers, in full stride; they wake like people brought back from cardiac arrest or from drowning: *in medias res*, surrounded by familiar people and objects, equipped with a hundred skills. They know the neighborhood, they can read and write English, they are old hands at the commonplace mysteries, and yet they feel themselves to have just stepped off the boat, just converged with their bodies, just flown down from a trance, to lodge in an eerily familiar life already well under way."

We begin our thinking about life in the middle, not at the beginning nor at the end. At the same time, like children, when we grow older we become curious about our beginnings and a little anxious about our ending. It is well to remember this when we ask questions about the beginning and ending of life. We are at best probing a mystery, not proving a theory.

So it is when we turn to the Bible—we are always at the middle. Even the account of the creation of the world and of the first humans was written, so it seems, by Moses who first of all discovered God as a redeemer, and only subsequently as a creator. Moses experienced the actual event of God's redemptive act in the liberation of his people from Egypt. He only thought about the origins of life, by divine inspiration you might say. Yes, but he could only then think about it after some years of experience. He could not literally go back to the beginning.

It would seem that we are guided toward the kind of thinking that begins with actuality and only then moves toward possibility. Knowledge of God began with the actuality of God's work in the redemption of humanity. Only from this 'center' can we think about the origins and the final destiny of human life. As Karl Barth liked to say, when it comes to our knowledge of God, the act of God reveals the being of God. We cannot think about God's being until we have encountered the act of God; even then, our thinking must be limited to and grounded in what can be known of God through his actions.

In somewhat the same way, we can only think about the

beginning of human life from the perspective of the concrete reality of what human is actually like. To project what we know as truly "human" backward into sheer biological material may be to think beyond what we actually know and border on the absurd. In the same way, to project what we know as truly "human" forward into some kind of post mortal form of life can become equally absurd. Even the Apostle Paul can only allude to the form of human life beyond death as veiled in a metaphor. The resurrection body will be somewhat like the form of a "bare seed," as a kernel of wheat. It is sown perishable and raised imperishable. It is sown a physical body and raised a spiritual body (1 Cor. 15:35-49).

From this perspective I suggest that there is what one might call a "middle zone" of human morality which defines and sustains human life from the center outwards, rather than from the beginning forward. From this middle zone we can recognize that which is human and that which is only potentially human as under our moral responsibility. That which we determine to be human we give a personal name, and even baptize.

Pastor John Stoneking published an article in the Methodist journal Circuit Rider (March, 1984) titled: "Would I Baptize a Stillborn Baby?" Called to the hospital by a potential grandmother whose daughter-in-law was about to give birth to a baby which had suddenly died in the womb, he pondered his pastoral responsibility and role. The grandmother wanted the stillborn baby baptized. The son and daughter-in-law had been married in the church three years previously but had never attended. Nothing in his seminary training had prepared him for this. He realized that this was no longer just a fetus, but would be a fully formed infant, though born dead.

As he waited with the family while labor was induced, he inquired as to whether or not they wanted to name the baby. They did, and as the dead and already decomposing baby was taken in his arms, he baptized the infant, in the "midst of tears, which is an authentic Baptism by water and the Spirit." A few minutes later, one of the grandparents said, "I assume that the baby will be gotten rid of by the hospital." Absolutely not, was his reply, "This baby must not disappear, but have a proper place in history," and then followed up with a simple graveside service.

This anecdote is not primarily about the legality of baptism from the perspective of church polity, but about the status of a stillborn fetus as a human person. From the "middle zone" of life this stillborn infant was a recognizable child, and was given a name. Would the pastor have baptized an embryo in a petri dish simply because some want to call this a "child" who needs to be adopted? I doubt it. I hope not.

My point is this. How far can we retreat from the center of human life and still recognize and affirm that the life form we observe is truly "human?" Yes, one can say that an embryo, whose life is sustained even in a freezer, is potentially human. But so is human sperm and a human ovum potentially human. The bioethics professor will establish a critical boundary called "viability." But as a concept of life this is also a slippery concept, not easily held in hand.

Decisions have to be made. From a middle zone moral perspective such decisions are difficult and often tragic, but they are still human decisions before they are ethical decisions. Before we can ask about what we *ought* to do ethically about human life, we need to determine what we mean by *human* life. Only those who are already human can make these decisions, though impinging on these decisions are scientific and ethical (political) factors and concerns.

Some years ago a woman gave birth to what appeared to be twins, two infants joined at the body, with two heads, but with only one heart. The heart sustained the vital organs of each through a network of veins and arteries. From a scientific perspective the situation required surgery if either were to survive, where the heart would be given to the one most likely to survive, the other simply disposed of as not viable as long as it had no heart. From an ethical position, the argument was made that such surgery was virtually murder, as it meant the intentional killing of one in order that the other might survive.

The scientific argument prevailed, one assumed with the consent of the parents caught in this tragic situation, and the two were separated, one left alive, the other dead. As it turned out, the one with the heart only survived a few weeks.

The case is now a study in medical ethics for future scholars to debate and divide. If one were to ask the parents, who live in the middle zone of human life, they would likely say that they had two children, Meagon and Mary, who both died shortly after birth. They regularly and reverently tend their graves as part of the history of their family life.

In the end, once the surgeons and the ethicists have departed, one is left with the question, did the parents do the right thing? I would argue that they did, not only in supporting the decision to save one human life (a tragic moral choice), but in affirming both as persons who were conceived, born and died (an authentic human choice).

I would find it difficult to question the act of the parents in making this decision on purely ethical grounds, as though the reality of this tragic confusion could be neatly (surgically!) separated by considering it primarily as an abstract question of right or wrong. In the case of upholding human life, the criteria are more ambiguous than ethicists like to think, but more precise than the scientists can measure. In some cases one must simply do the right thing because it is the decent thing to do.

Often parents will say to their children who are involved in some activity, "Stop it! That's not nice." Or, "Stop it! That's not good for you." Or, "Stop it! That's not decent."

One of the enigmatic texts of Scripture (and there are many) is the injunction given by Moses: "Do not boil a kid in its mother's milk!" The warning is given three times (Exodus 23:19; 34:26; Deut. 14:21) with little or no context to suggest why such an act would be wrong. If one were to ask Moses I suspect that he would simply say, "because it would be indecent to do so." The violation is not one based on medical or moral grounds, but on human sensibility. Some things are just not right because they offend our sense of decency. This is middle zone morality. We live by it, we teach our children by it, and we hold each other accountable to it.

Indecency is not first of all an abstract ethical or even legal concept; it is a middle zone moral concept which people understand clearly as relating to the protection of that which is personal and therefore human.

My former professor of philosophical theology, Edward John Carnell, suggested something similar to what I call a middle zone moral sense. Children, argued Carnell, possess an inner and accurate sense of virtue and of right and wrong, though they do not always live by it. Nor are they able to articulate the basis for their moral judgment; they just *know* what is to be expected of a good person. "Happy children bear witness to the release that love brings. Though they may suffer a great deal, they do not despair, for love dissolves fear. . . . Happy children are so full of love that they extend overtures of fellowship in every direction. . . The whole world is a kingdom of love." As a result, Carnell says, children have an intuitive perception of virtue. "When adults are asked to tell what virtue is, they often give the impression that the task is beyond their capacity.. . . If happy children were to hear of this, they might be somewhat amused, for they discover the meaning of virtue by listening to their own hearts."

What Carnell says about the intuitive moral sense of love as reflected in happy children is true of humanity in general, despite the repression of this moral sense in favor of actions based on self gratification or on a need to gain power over one's own life or the lives of others.

The conception and birth of one of our grandsons was the result of in vitro fertilization. Our daughter and her husband chose to use this method to give birth to a child in a situation which otherwise was impossible. This "happy child," to use Carnell's phrase, came into being and lived in this middle zone of human life, where there was no ethical crisis in making the decision. There was no need to say, "stop it!" On the other hand, if someone were to use this medical procedure merely to produce human embryos for sale or to use for a purpose other than to create life, enhance life or to serve as good for others, I might well say "stop it!" There is a point at which something which is good in and of itself, can become "indecent" when performed without regard to the borderline that runs right through our humanity. "Love does no wrong to a neighbor," wrote the Apostle Paul. "Therefore love is the fulfilling of the law" (Romans 13:10).

To call an embryo in a petri dish a child which needs to be adopted, offends my sense of what we mean by speaking of a human person. On the other hand—yes, there are two hands!—my sensibility is equally offended by referring to a living, viable fetus in a mother's womb as merely human tissue. I think that we ought to know better. I often get the impression that those who take a "pro life" position and those who take a "pro choice" position regarding the abortion issue each have their hand raised in the air trying to make their point, but the hands do not clasp one another so as to hold the mystery and miracle of human life at the center.

From the middle zone, theologically, I would argue that being a human person demands a sufficient biological form of life to sustain viability. At the same time, while biological life form is a necessity for human life, it is by itself not sufficient. Technically this means that human life is not biologically determined but contingent upon a source and power beyond mere biological life. The Scripture tells us that we are taken from the dust of the ground, as are all other creatures, but that God "breathed the breath of life" into these life forms and they became human persons, not merely creatures (Genesis 2).

Solidarity with other creatures at one level does not entail belonging at another. Humans simply do not *belong* to the animal world. This is common sense at the middle zone of life. The biblical story of creation gives us an answer as to why this is so from a theological perspective. God has determined and continues to determine, I would argue, that the difference between the human and nonhuman is not one of biological degree but of qualitative life form.

Years ago, when surgeons at Loma Linda hospital in California transplanted a heart from a baby baboon into the body of "baby Sue," I gave a sermon on the subject, suggesting that we should accept the fact that humans have a strong solidarity and likeness at the biological level with non human creatures, but that when the heart of an animal was surgically placed into the heart of a human infant, it became a human heart, so to speak.

To speak of a "human heart" obviously required a kind of middle zone understanding that to use the heart of an animal to sustain human life is a human act and ought not offend our sensibilities. To perform a reverse kind of operation, though scientifically possible, would violate our sensibilities and be an inhuman act. Is this not a sufficient basis on which to make a decision?

Those who differ might argue that this is a very subjective way of thinking and creates the so-called "slippery slope" by which anything could be allowed. My response is that nothing is more objective than the actuality of human being and human life. And that if we begin with the middle zone, we are beginning with objective reality, not merely subjective theory.

A former student, a woman then in her late 40s, wrote a paper for me in which she told of an incident in her own life as a way of thinking out the moral and theological implications of a decision she made. Through amniocentesis, she discovered that the fetus which she was carrying was microcephalic and neurologically damaged to the point that it could not survive more than a few hours or a few days at best following birth. With counseling from her parish minister, she and her husband agreed to a therapeutic abortion. She described the experience in this way.

> As the doctor infused my uterus with a natural hormone designed to bring on labor, I felt so terribly sad, yet very much at peace. That peace sustained me as a very difficult labor ensured. I took no anesthetic, because I wanted to experience this child as I had experienced my others. When the child came, I felt tiny legs kicking my legs, and

> I asked the nurse to hand me my baby. She cut the cord and put the little girl on my breast with great tenderness. She tried to breathe and I held her as she left this life and went on to Him. She was a person. She was conceived in love and created by God. She deserved to be treated with utmost respect and humility. For she was an enigma, as are all of us who are persons. . . . The nurse who sensed my need understood what I was doing. We did not have the church's liturgy that day, but her own enactment served the same purpose. She was held in love as the transition from this life to eternal life was made.

Those who read this will have a variety of responses. Some will be outraged and horrified with such an act. Others will question the act based on ethical grounds, arguing that this was no different than murdering the child. Some may understand and accept what she did without having any justification for it. This is a middle zone human decision. An intervention was made for the sake of claiming the humanity of this child in the face of the grotesque and inhuman genetic accident which produced such malformation at the biological level.

When does human life begin, and when does it end?

From the middle, we cannot see completely to the end, though we are always drawn towards it by the occurrence of death. Even then, there is ambiguity and uncertainty from a scientific and ethical perspective. Cell division in a corpse continues for a time after certification of death is written, I am told. This is a biological form of life, though it is so attenuated that what we recognize as human life in terms of brain function no longer exists. Decisions are made, giving us permission, even demanding, that we no longer view the remains as a human person but a human body, to be treated with respect even as it is surrendered back to the earth from which it came.

The death of young boy who was diabetic resulted from withdrawal of insulin by his parents under the assumption that he had been miraculously healed by a visiting preacher. The scientific fact of his death did not deter the parents from their conviction that God would raise him from the dead. Failing to see God act in response to their prayers for healing, they felt that he was testing their faith and they scheduled a resurrection service for the dead boy, even after an autopsy had been performed. At this point, even the pastor of the church and the members who had supported the claim for healing turned away. The parents ended up alone at the graveside calling out to God for a miracle, even as the body of their dead son lay in the coffin. Those who learned of this incident, later made into a TV film, were rightly appalled at the lengths to which the parents went in refusing to accept the reality of death. While they were arrested and charged and convicted of child neglect, the deeper conviction of the community, from the middle zone, as it were, was that their actions, and their faith, offended human sensibility.

It might seem irrational to some that Christians hold the conviction that following physical death human persons continue to live before God in a spiritual form, even with a resurrected body. This is the bold claim of the New Testament with regard to the question of what happens after death. As a component of Christian faith, the claim does not violate our sensibilities, though it may challenge the limits of our intellectual and scientific knowledge.

As life slips away toward death, we reach as far as we can from the middle toward this mysterious and foreboding event when it happens to others. I say that we reach as far as we can, for our human reach goes further than we can see or understand scientifically or ethically. On occasion, we let go of a fellow human for the sake of his or her humanity, though medical science and ethics might urge us to delay death so far as possible. There is a sense in which we need permission to die more than a right to die.

I came to understand this more fully, not in a theological classroom but as a new pastor when the father of a young boy who had been critically injured in a bicycle accident called me to the hospital on a Sunday afternoon. The father was also a medical doctor, attending our church, and was the attending physician.

He explained to me the situation. The boy had been put on

a ventilator and by this means was kept breathing. The father put his hand on the head of his son and told me that his brain had been injured beyond repair and that death was inevitable. He also said that with the artificial breathing apparatus and other medical devices and service he could keep him alive for weeks, perhaps months.

He then asked me to consider with him the fact that this boy was already on his way to live forever with God and that we were only holding back this transition. We could not restore his life, he told me, we could only delay his death. With that, he suggested taking one more EEG reading and if the results indicated brain death, removing the ventilator and allowing him to die. We prayed together, he performed the procedure, and then removed the ventilator, holding the struggling limbs of his son as he passed from this life to the next.

I realized that I was an accomplice to an act for which I had, at that time, no theological or, perhaps, ethical grounds for justification. At the same time, I felt that his was a deeply human and responsible act taken not only by a professional medical technician but by a parent. At the graveside, as I concluded the service of interment, the father asked for the casket to be opened, withdrew a letter from his pocket and placed it on the breast of his son. He then told the assembled group that he had written a letter to his son, explaining not only what he had done but also why he had done this, with assurance of a reunion in heaven.

The father had reached as far as he could from the middle zone of life toward that boundary which separates this life from the next. He did not push back that boundary, using scientific technology in fear of ethical malfeasance. Instead, he performed a final human act, both in the hospital room as well as at the graveside for his son.

My life began in the middle zone. I hope that it will end there as well, surrounded by those who will preserve my humanity by releasing me from the inhumanity and indecency of prolonged dying. Think about it!

Musings of a Maverick Theologian

> In a world of fugitives
> One who moves in the opposite direction
> Will appear to run away.
> [J. G. Hamann]

Those who protest the stretching of the mind through the communication of the gospel, and insist that one must speak "simply" like Jesus did, find no justification for this intellectual barrenness in Scripture. Jesus constantly prefaced his teaching with the challenge "What do you think?" There is a temptation to probe the complacency of those who sit week after week in church under the preaching of the Word with the question, "What do you use your brain for?" And yet, perhaps those who listen would like the courage to ask the same question of those of us who speak the Word of God!

⁂

Whether one speaks **in** a tongue or speaks **with** a tongue, I cannot help but agree with Paul who said, "I would rather speak five words with my mind, in order to instruct others also, than ten thousand words in a tongue" (1 Corinthians 14:19). One of the great truths of redemptive love is the inspiration of the human mind by the action of the Spirit of God. Paul intimates that we can "think the thoughts of God" through the prompting of the personality by the Spirit of God (1 Corinthians 2:11-12).

⁂

Dietrich Bonhoeffer, who left the security of his office as a German pastor to enter the conspiracy against Hitler, once said, "What is worse than doing evil is being evil. It is worse for a liar to tell the truth than of a lover of truth to lie."

The lover of truth is basically an honest person who has demonstrated a consistent pattern of truthfulness in word and deed. The liar is basically a dishonest person who will use the truth to deceive and manipulate others.

When evil appears in the form of truth, we are blinded to its moral danger because we ordinarily assume that behind true words is an honest person. This is why it is worse for a liar to tell the truth. The liar counts on our commitment to take a person at his or her word until proven otherwise. By that time, it is too late. The liar has deceived us by telling the truth and gaining this advantage over us.

When an honest person, for one reason or another, is caught in a lie, we immediately note the contradiction because we know the person to be basically honest in word and deed. When the lie is acknowledged and forgiveness sought, the virtue of honesty remains intact despite the lapse. If deception becomes a pattern and the telling of lies flagrant, then we would finally revise our judgment of the person's character because the virtue of honesty no longer is evident.

If an evil person deceives us by using truth as a tactic for gaining our trust so as to do us harm, the act of deception reveals a basically dishonest person. We are more vulnerable to evil disguised as truth because in such a person there is no virtue of honesty to which we can appeal in looking for repentance and recompense.

⁂

We do not use language, language uses us, wrote Heidegger. Being comes to us, he said, not through the words alone, but through the spaces which words create. Too often we close these spaces with the cement of logic so that no meaning can leak out. In doing so, we are plastering the inside of our own tomb.

⁂

I do not believe that Jesus Christ is the answer to a "God-shaped vacuum" in the human heart, as a philosopher once put it. This is a nice text for a sophomore in a Christian college who is searching for an intellectual argument for the experience of God. The problem with a vacuum is that it is indiscriminate and will draw in anything that is floating around in the air.

I am more attracted to the wisdom of Michael Polanyi who once wrote, "Our believing is conditioned at its source by our belonging." Psychologists tell us that forming early attachments, called bonding, is an essential basis for healthy and effective personal relationships in life. Jesus said, "where two or three are gathered in my name, I am there among them" (Matt 18:20). I grew up with a strong sense of belonging. I have never had trouble believing.

※※※※※※

We always know more than we can tell. There is a knowledge at the core of the self for which we will never find words. It rises up within us without our bidding and cannot be forgotten or erased by the most strenuous act of the will nor by the most delirious ecstasy of emotion.

In the bond of love and attachment experienced by the first man and woman, each has a knowledge of the absence of the other. In the pleasure of life's most gratifying moments, there is a knowledge of the passing away of that life, and that is death. In the most self-assured managing of one's possessions in life, there is the knowledge of their impending loss.

※※※※※※

The grace of God must first kill before it can make alive. It was the barrenness of Sarah, not the virility of Abraham, that produced the promised seed. When we forget that, there is an Ishmael that cannot be comforted and an Esau who weeps to no avail.

※※※※※※

Jesus played no favorites!

He ignored the categories established within his own society. For him the despised Samaritan was a woman who could give <u>him</u> a drink, the self righteous Pharisee a man who wanted to talk, the leper a person who needed to be touched.

While people came to him in bunches, needs came with a

name. A congregation was not a mob to send home to eat, but individuals to be fed with bread broken with his own hands. In a crowd he was never simply pushed by people, but touched by someone who hurt. Within the shouting sounds of a multitude he heard the cry of the blind man, the sigh of a sinner, the murmur of a skeptic. He let people be like who they were and offered to help them become who could be. He had no uniforms for his disciples and no masks for his friends. He did not ask for conformity but for commitment. His style was love, his pattern devotion.

※※※※※

Jesus said, "Where your treasure is, there will your heart be also (Matthew 6:21). Would we be wrong in reversing it and say—where your heart is, there will your treasure be also? He did counsel a rich man to "sell what you have and give to the poor, and you will have treasure in heaven" (Matthew 19:21). He did insist by parable that the uninvested talent be taken from the one and given to the other who had multiplied his through use (Matthew 25).

The increasing complaint that life is empty and unrewarding cannot be justified by circumstances alone. The answer is unmistakable, even if unpalatable—we each must be the major investors in our own life. The depressed are robbers of temples—expecting to gain what they do not give. The chronic complainers are misers—demanding room service without paying the bill. The skeptics are misanthropes—scanning the horizon of humanity with distorted lens. The bored are parasites—waiting for the inspiration of others to provide a vicarious thrill.

※※※※※

We are easy prey for the comfort of convenience. The challenge to follow Christ is felt by many to be an invasion of personal freedom. The imperative of Christian ministry becomes an interruption of the indispensable routine. It is unfortunate, but true, that the highest motivation among Christians often is the opportunity which is made the most convenient. Not the least of Jesus' sufferings was the "inconvenience of the cross."

I protest the comfort of complacency that editorializes profoundly on distant atrocities, while the crippled crawl beneath the closed windows of compassion. Jesus wept over Jerusalem, not Rome. He followed his tears into the streets where others knew his discomfort. Strangely, in his distress, the hope of humanity recognized the heart of God—and they were not wrong.

※※※※※※

If there are two sides to humanity, Jesus will often be found on the wrong side. This is a scandal to the righteous, but pleasing to God.

※※※※※※

The justice of God does not require the suspension of grace, despite what some moralists say. In the final judgment, God may give the parents of the man who murdered both his father and his mother permission to decide his eternal fate. If they should seek reconciliation rather than retaliation, who will claim that an injustice has been done?

※※※※※※

Those who lack the virtue of generosity suffer a spiritual deficit. Their own spirit is cramped and crushed, like an eagle caged in a zoo. Lacking the freedom to soar its spirit turns sour and surly. Stalking the boundaries of its limited existence, the fettered spirit misinterprets the freedom of others as prodigality, and becomes miserly and mean. It is the meanness of spirit, not the habit of miserliness, that marks the spiritual deficit in the ungenerous.

Fearing the bonding of spirit with another as a form of bondage, those who lack the spirit of generosity retaliate when they are wounded and are impatient with the suffering of others. The ungenerous spirit maintains its freedom from the demands of others by cutting the cords of human compassion and declaring resident alien status in the human family.

※※※※※※

As a boy growing up on a farm in the Midwest, I spent many hours alone, often in the fields with the animals, but also choosing my own special places to spend some hours. In those experiences, I recall a feeling of wonderment and a sense of timelessness.

The membrane that separated my inner self from the larger world that pressed in upon me grew porous. The familiar sights and sounds that filled my everyday world had cracks in them through which the vast and mysterious unknown breathed upon me, filling my soul with a knowledge for which there were no names and a language for which there were no words. I still can hear, if I listen, the cry of wild geese winging their way across the night which awakened this small boy and left him staring into the dark, not wanting them to fly out of my hearing. But after they disappeared, I lay there wondering what to do with the infinite silence which they left in their wake.

⚜⚜⚜⚜⚜

Intimacy is the intensification of otherness.

In a sermon preached in London on May 27, 1934, Dietrich Bonhoeffer said: "The greatest mystery to us is not the one furthest away but the one closest to us . . . It is the final depth of everything mysterious when two people come so close one to the other than they *love* each other . . . The more they love each other and in that love know one of the other, the more profoundly they discern the mystery of their love. Thus, knowing does not dissolve mystery but deepens it. *That* the other is close to me, that is the greatest mystery." The awareness of the **self** of the other as absolutely standing over and against our own self is like an electric shock. The experiences shared which seemed to draw two people together as having 'something in common,' now reveal a confrontation with the mystery and spirit of another self which is totally other than one's own self. The shared intimacy of communication and communion intensifies the **otherness** of each.

⚜⚜⚜⚜⚜

The boy thrust his hand deep into the freshly plowed soil. "This soil is your life," his father suddenly said. "You take care of it and it will take care of you."

Years later, having left the soil, and his father, he discovered the wisdom of his father's words. His father had not bound his hand to the soil, but his hand to his heart. Now, wherever he thrusts his hand, he finds his heart—and his father.

⚜⚜⚜⚜⚜⚜

I am no 'Pollyanna' who insists that there is a silver lining in every storm cloud. There's a lot of wind and rain in some of those clouds. I have watched the driving hail strip the growing corn down to the naked stalk and walked amidst the havoc wrought by the savage wind unleashed upon the golden grain. I have swallowed hard and suffered in silence when forced to accept less than I thought I deserved. There have been times when my own foolishness, or carelessness, rose up to mock me and demand the 'pound of flesh' which never satisfied the ravenous hunger of shame. I too have grieved the death of youthful dreams, have bid farewell to unfulfilled ambitions, and kept my promise when doing so closed other doors which offered fulfillment of what was desired above all.

These experiences are not unknown to persons who are the possessors of happiness. Happy are those who have the strength to bear weakness, who have the courage to face their fears, and whose embrace of life enlarges through every loss.

⚜⚜⚜⚜⚜⚜

Jesus was not only raised from the grave; he was also raised from hell. In the deepest caverns of the abyss, there is the sign of the cross, and it is empty.

⚜⚜⚜⚜⚜⚜

Writing to his friend from a prison cell, Dietrich Bonhoeffer, the German pastor and theologian, reflected upon a quotation from Girodano Bruno that stuck in his mind: "There can be something frightening about the sight of a friend; no enemy can be so terrifying as he." Bonhoeffer added: "Does 'terrifying' refer to the inherent danger of betrayal, inseparable from close intimacy. . . ?" There is indeed something 'terrifying' as well as exhilarating about the encounter with another whose spirit is open to ours. When this moment of vulnerability and exposure to the spirit of another occurs, it is an unavoidable experience of intimacy. We are not often prepared for it and shrink from its implications. But this retreat from intimacy dissolves the other into a safe, but distant, counterpart to ourselves.

※※※※※

Faith is not the bridge we build to get to God—that is folly!—but it is creating a path for God to come to us.

Faith and folly are sibling rivals, growing up in the same household, but not cut out of the same cloth. Folly may be likened to the weeds which grow amidst the wheat, appearing at early stages to be quite similar. It is only at harvest, said Jesus, that the wheat can be separated as it has produced a full head of grain (Matthew 13:24-30).

Folly has two step sisters, greed and grandiosity. Grandiosity, psychologists tell us, is the illusion that one is greater than one really is, leading to delusions of self importance and success. Greed, of course, is the insatiable desire to accumulate things for the sake of gaining power and security.

Folly manufactures evidence where there is none, while faith sees evidence that is not visible. Folly is the attempt to "make visible" what is unreal and so elicit commitment from others and give oneself permission to satisfy greed and grandiosity. Faith envisions what is real, though not visible, while folly makes visible what is unreal.

※※※※※

Love is not a torrent of water unleashed down the side of a mountain, but Love is a steady flow of water through a channel which irrigates a field. The river which graces the land with life-sustaining water becomes a devastating and destructive force when it overflows its boundaries. What makes a river is not the passivity of its current, but that its passion is kept within bounds.

Love without passion is anemic and sterile. The famous Dead Sea in Palestine is so called because it has no outlet. Eventually the salts and minerals in the water make it inhospitable for living organisms. When love dies and loses its passion it not only becomes sterile but toxic.

⚜⚜⚜⚜⚜

The love of God is portrayed as well by God's passionate anger as well as by his solicitous and searching care. God's passionate love is like a fierce warrior who has righteous anger at that which demeans or destroys the object of love. But the passion in that anger is well aimed and not merely well armed. Its aim is accurate and its focus is narrow and laser-like in its clean and cutting edge.

Where the passion of love is without the boundary of purpose it becomes indiscriminate, promiscuous and fatal. The passion of love can produce giddiness as well as gladness. Love that rides the crest of passion's wave becomes merely "high surf," and we must remember that waves reach their crest only when they are about to crash on shore.

⚜⚜⚜⚜⚜

Hope requires risk, so much that it creates expectations beyond our reach. Hope makes us vulnerable to future and even greater loss. Hope exposes us to disappointment, frustration and betrayal. Faith plants the seed and promises a harvest, and so creates hope. But with the promise of a harvest comes the possibility that the promise will fail. That is the betrayal that hope must bear. Without faith as the investment of one's precious life and resources in the power of life, the burden of hope could not be borne. But faith bears that burden in partnership with hope, for it is partnership with God, the author and creator of life.

⚜⚜⚜⚜⚜

I peer at the black and white pictures, now yellowing with age, taken by my parents during those early years, and gaze with curiosity and wonder at the child I see that bears my name. Even these pictures stir no memory. All of those delicious, terrifying, comforting, exciting, tastes, sounds, smells and touches lie buried in some inaccessible vault while I still search for the key. I remember the smell of tobacco smoke in my father's clothes, and the comforting feel of his work-worn hands as a boy of six, but not of his tender touch and soft voice when he played with me as a toddler learning to walk. Is it a blessing or a tragedy that we do not remember the experiences of our early childhood?

※※※※※

His name is Brogan. He is twenty months old, and he is my grandson. We play in the park, feed the ducks, and pretend that he is running away and I can barely run fast enough to catch him. He calls me Papa, and for just a brief moment looks into my eyes with undisguised love and trust. It was, for me at least, and I think for him, an experience that psychologists call bonding. Like two gulls swooping across a sunlit meadow, our winged souls touched in flight. We both sensed the presence of the other and felt the sudden stab of recognition that yields a pleasure almost too painful to bear.

Then it struck me. He will not remember this moment nor hold for long the image of my face in his mind. For a few weeks perhaps, aided by a picture and some parental prompting, he will give the correct answer when quizzed about name and face.

When we meet again I will enter his familiar world as a stranger and we will need to become friends once again. Yes I know, the bonding may well be there, the psychologists tell me. But I want Brogan to tell me! I want him to remember, not just my face, but his own feelings of shared joy and love. When he is older, I will tell him the story, of course, and he will believe it. But he will not likely ever recover the feelings that became so much a part of the self that he now recognizes as his own. When he awakens to himself, like all of us, he will ponder the mystery of those years between his birth and his awakening. Part of the self remains silent and never speaks, no matter how fluent the vocabulary of the mind.

※※※※※

Children are not born with courage because they have not yet learned fear.

Fearlessness is the armor which shame wears when it goes forth to seize another prize to exhibit in the inner room called despair. Every encounter must be a conquest, and every lover a trophy. Each time that shame is felt over the price one must pay to bring love to the side of fear, the armor of fearlessness is quickly assumed. When love attempts to cast out the hidden fear and heal the shame, it is love that is cast out, fear remains. These people are brave and beautiful, in their own eyes. They are pictures of sadness and sorrow for those who love and lament.

Fearlessness is not the absence of fear. Fearlessness is fear in its full dress uniform seeking a parade and a prize. In attempting to be fearless, one seeks to overcome fear by feeding it with the illusion of power and invulnerability.

Courage is more humble and far more realistic. It accepts fear as a necessary part of life. Without courage, fear would never permit us to open the door to life and love. It takes courage to hope and to have faith when we know fear. It takes courage to live with our weaknesses, our vulnerability, our loneliness. It takes courage to live with fear.

⚜⚜⚜⚜⚜

Why does it seem easier to show kindness to a friend than to one's marriage partner? When persons who are married do not show kindness as a consistent pattern, the marriage is no longer a caring and loving one. Such a marriage has failed the litmus test of love. For love is not a relation where one only takes care **of** the other, but where both take care **for** the other. When one becomes incapacitated and unable to care for oneself, taking care of the other become the deepest expression of love. The promise of love includes the commitment to the care of each other should the need arise. But mutual care for each other is what keeps lovers friends and produces the fruit of kindness.

⚜⚜⚜⚜⚜

Happiness is not the gentle stroke of good luck, nor is it the sensuous power of success. Good luck sets us up for the sucker punch of a blow to the solar plexus at the moment we have raised our hands above our heads in praise to the gods of fortune and fame. Success is a miserable companion on the way to the top and a fair-weather friend on the way down.

❋❋❋❋❋

The Japanese Haiku probed my heart with particular poignancy:

> Seeing my birth-cord
> kept at our old
> native place...
> New Year's day I wept.

Whence these tears? For the security of childhood too long forgotten? Or for the tragedy of being born? It could well be both, for tears are never simple things nor life an open book.

I do know this. We spend the greater part of early life attempting to throw off the cocoon of birth and adolescence. There is an unreasonable urge to escape the influence and structures of our nativity, longing for the bright wings of individuality and unhindered self-expression. I fear that our age has made this urge a privilege, if not a demand. With dispassionate skill, the therapist enters in to probe the agonizing core of one's being until the new self emerges, freed from the traumas of parental love gone awry. Healing from old wounds is necessary, but where is the birth-cord?

The stewardship of life is a gift to us, and if we have despised this birthright, we would do well to weep for the birth-cord of our nativity. These are good tears.

❋❋❋❋❋

He cradled the rifle in his arms, on a cold winter morning. Suddenly a red fox, surprised by his silent approach, froze in fear. Crouching only a short distance away beside a snow covered shock of corn, the fox stared into his eyes with a fear that he came to understand as that which bound him to the creature, for that brief moment in time. Only when he finally shuffled his feet did the animal release him from the compelling power of that common knowledge and bounded away. The gun was never raised; his aim was no longer to kill.

❋❋❋❋❋

There are flowers that bloom near every tomb. And if it seems strange that life should flaunt its color so close to darkness, then one has missed both the sense of death and the secret of life. To the one who observes, earth promises us more than it takes from us. That our destiny on earth is in the dust from which we came cannot be doubted. It is only the spirit in us that fears the darkness. The power of the soil to produce life out of death is a parable of hope to the human heart. Yet, hope soon stumbles over its own ignorance and with Job, whispers the doubt that follows every soul, "If a man dies shall he live again?"

The flowers of a thousand generations have never opened a tomb nor lighted its darkness into life. These are only feeble intimations of a stillborn truth. The odor of death is scarcely masked by the fragrance of life—flowers bloom outside of the tomb, not within it. Let flowers bloom close to every tomb. And if it seems strange that life should be so bold in death, then remember, there is one tomb with living flowers in it.

I go there occasionally to smell its fragrance.

⚜⚜⚜⚜⚜⚜

"They heard the sound of the Lord God walking in the garden at the time of the evening breeze" (Genesis 3:8).

It is a lonely garden that has fragrance without sound. The esthetic thrill of well-kept borders guarding exotic plants soon gives way to a longing for friendly footsteps anticipating response. Those who make beauty their divinity shall be haunted by inescapable silence. It is easier to clothe ourselves in the familiarity of the daily routine than to acknowledge the sound of divinity leading the heart into new echoes of response. We disguise ourselves behind the facade of friendliness and scarcely permit the intimacy of friendship to become a spiritual reality. It is more comfortable to talk of theology than faith; safer to make small talk than reveal deep feelings.

The voice of God always speaks our name and that is how we recognize the sound of divinity.

⚜⚜⚜⚜⚜⚜

"If you and daddy die, then we will only need two placemats at our table," our 5 year old grandson said to his mother. Two placemats, one for him and one for his brother. A visual image used to tame the terror of an unspeakable fear. Who will care for us? This is the question we dare not ask, but can never forget.

✤✤✤✤✤

"Teacher, I brought you my son; he has a spirit that makes him unable to speak." (Mark 9:17). The distressed father who brought his afflicted son to Jesus for healing identified the boy's malady as having an "inarticulate spirit." The older translations called it a "dumb spirit."

"How long has he had this?" asked Jesus. "From childhood," replied the father. "It has often cast him into the fire and to the water, to destroy him... if you are able... help us."

From childhood. Of course! Here is where our tentative movements into relationships are sometimes stillborn, and we withdraw into the security of acting out our life rather than experiencing it. This is why we can move with facility in a technical world that is satisfied with proficiency, and care little that we so often appear to have a "dumb spirit"—or care even less that others appear to be speaking without making sounds.

Absorbed in the mechanics of living, the windows of the self become steamed over with our daily breath—we cannot see out, nor others in. Bound with inhibitions we take refuge in a vocabulary of vacuities. Where there are no conversations from the heart there are often convulsions of the spirit. In our inarticulate rage, we flail and flounder, falling into the fire and the water. Wordlessly, the rescue continues its relentless cycle. Despair is dumb but dutiful. Is a cure possible?

The strange voice we hear is our own. The barrenness of busyness forces the heart to protest its exclusion from the reality of relationship. Estrangement is an aching abyss that lies unresponsive to the ministrations of bright immediacies. Despair is akin to faith, and feeling to being. Compelled from within, the mind dares to ask the question for which the heart

has long sought an answer—If you are able!"
I would like to have heard the boy speak.

※※※※※※

One definition of the grace of God says that it is 'unmerited favor.' That is true, but it tends to focus on our undeservedness. To receive as a gift what we have not earned is truly a blessing of grace and an expression of love. At the same time, because grace has its source in love, what love promises when it makes the other an object of love **creates** in the loved one an expectation of a blessing. We have not merited this blessing, but it is rightfully ours because it has been promised by love.

※※※※※※

Fear is like fatigue. When the muscle is able to relax, the fatigue disappears. The self is like a muscle. It contracts and reacts to stimulation through feeling. The feeling does not go anywhere when the fear disappears. Rather, the feeling releases its grip on the fear and "lets go." This is why feeling itself is capable of restoration and recovery when negative and painful sensations are replaced by positive and supportive ones.

※※※※※※

My father used to plant potatoes every Spring. First we would cut them into pieces, making sure that each piece had an "eye" in it, as he called it. From this "eye" a sprout would form and then the pieces were ready to be placed in the ground. One thing remained, however, before we could plant. To ensure a good harvest of potatoes, my father said, we must plant them when the moon is full. So we would wait until the propitious time, and then place them in the ground.

We always had sufficient potatoes, come Fall, as I recall. In those days, I did not venture to submit this folk wisdom to a scientific test by deliberately planting some during another phase of the moon. I doubt that he did either. It was probably the only superstition that I recall my father ever including in his otherwise common sense approach to the tilling of the soil and the husbandry of our livestock.

Even as I write this, why do I feel a sense of uneasiness in making such a clear distinction between superstition and common sense? He would not have been happy with such a charge. For him, the working of the soil was a participation in a cycle of sowing and reaping, suffering crop failures and rejoicing at bountiful harvests. He never disclosed his inner feelings, neither of grief at his losses nor of joy at his successes. I gather now that he lived a self-life in communion with the seasons of nature, with the rhythm of birth, life and death and, yes, by the phases of the moon! This may be the most common of all senses!

❧❧❧❧❧

Our deepest feelings are often invested in that which has the capacity to break our hearts. At the same time, it is necessary to make these risky investments in order to plant the seed of love in the soil of life. The risk of failure is no reason not to go forth and plant.

❧❧❧❧❧

We are each born with a deficit of love. We are deprived at the core of our being of the original blessing, and make impossible demands upon ourselves for fulfillment. This 'original sin' traps every person in the vicious circle of non-fulfillment. Despite every effort to make up for the deficit in the self through knowledge and awareness, we still find that we are prone to using and abusing others.

Some, meaning to save us from this condition, tell us that we are worthless, not merely hopeless. Only by denying ourselves, we are warned, can we be accepted by God's grace. We have no merit in ourselves, and no right to expect anything of God, so the evangelists tell us. This 'half-truth' of the gospel of grace can offer the gift of salvation, but ordinarily does not result in the full truth of being blessed! Look around, the church is filled with people who profess God's salvation from sin but are still searching for God's blessing of love. Not having received the blessing promised, many Christians still are looking for the 'pay-off' in serving God.

Fleeing from King Saul, lonely and isolated, "David said longingly, 'O that someone would give me water to drink from the well of Bethlehem that is by the gate.'" Three of David's 'mighty men,' hearing him speak, broke through the camp of the Philistines, drew water from the well in Bethlehem and brought it to David. "But he would not drink of it; he poured it out to the Lord, for he said, 'The Lord forbid that I should do this. Can I drink of the blood of the men who went at the risk of their lives?' Therefore he would not drink of it" (2 Samuel 23:13-17).

How many times have we sent people back to the well in Bethlehem in a misguided attempt to make us happy? How often have we drunk the water to satisfy a craving only to miss the blessing of a caring heart! We exchange the priceless longing for self fulfillment for the cheap currency of emotional needs. But the inflationary spiral of needs propels us into emotional bankruptcy, and we file for 'chapter 11' by retaining the services of a therapist. And if the therapist is wise, she will become a liturgist and, instead of handing us the water to drink, will empower us to pour it out 'to the Lord,' and thereby receive the blessing. We can teach therapists and counselors the skill of finding the well at Bethlehem, but the wisdom of knowing what to do with it when it is found, is an art known only to those who themselves know the blessing. When longing is fulfilled by love, it is strange how needs diminish.

A joyless life is one that has lost its sense of wonder.

Our sense of wonder is lost when our curiosity becomes clinical. We have an insatiable desire to explore, picking apart life like a young child so fascinated with how a toy works that he cannot resist taking it apart. Alas, he has discovered its secret but lost the joy of playing with it.

When our curiosity becomes too clinical the wonder is lost in life. It's bad enough when we become clinical about the way we feel, about the way we live, but when we become clinical about who we are and what the meaning of life is, we have passed out of the sanctuary into the laboratory.

We lose our sense of wonder when worship becomes self-analysis. The divine image in us is meant to be a lens through which we can discover the reality of God as well as the mystery of our own being, not a mirror in which we probe the secrets of our past. Worship is meant to be something that is directed away from us toward one who is our counterpart in every way, and yet stands outside of the boundaries of our human finitude and weakness.

Our sense of wonder is lost when the miraculous becomes routine. When the science of human behavior destroys the mythical life of the soul, life is sanitized of all sacredness. When the star which the wise men followed becomes a comet explained in an astronomy textbook, we have been given information but not inspiration.

※※※※※

Friendship may be the only form of human social relationships which is sustained primarily by kindness.

Kindness is the glue which binds friends together. If I should humiliate a friend, be insensitive to the feelings of a friend, cause unnecessary harm or hurt to a friend, or in any way treat a friend as an object that I use for my own pleasure and gratification, the friendship dissolves. There is no reason why a person should want to continue a friendship where there is no kindness, other than we use another to meet other needs. And in that case it is not a true and healthy friendship.

Kindness is the seed we plant in another's garden to grow fruit for our own enjoyment. When we care for the garden of another's life we are ensuring a harvest of fruit for our own pleasure. The proverb says it well: "Those who are kind reward themselves, but the cruel do themselves harm" (Proverbs 11:17).

※※※※※

The human spirit is the core of the self as desiring, cherishing, longing, and believing. As we grow and develop as persons, our spirit selects and assimilates from all of our experiences; it creates and colors life with the tension and texture which vibrates with urgency and reposes in peace. The spirit wills and resists, it opens and closes, it gives and receives. To share our spirit is to receive the other into the sacred shrine of what is most personal and dear; to share the spirit of the other is to be welcomed freely and trustingly into their holy of holies.

※※※※※

Compassion is only a feeling until it becomes an act of mercy. In showing mercy, one seeks to alleviate pain, temper justice, and restore relationships. While mercy is prompted by compassion, it has its source in the moral virtue of promoting the value of a human life when it least deserves it or cannot bear it. We applaud acts of mercy because we recognize the moral goodness of such actions which go beyond the legal demands of the law.

※※※※※

The brokenness of the human spirit is a deeper and more creative edge than guilt and remorse for sin. A sense of guilt is not creative and produces no positive motivation toward spiritual wholeness. We tend to forget that the cross of Christ only has significance as a place where sin is judged for those who have experienced the power of resurrection and the gift of the Spirit of God.

※※※※※

The cemetery adjoining my boyhood farm was separated from us by only a wire fence through which I easily could crawl back and forth. Having crossed over many times in my youthful play, I shall not be surprised to find myself crossing once more—for the last time—drawn by the view from the other side.

※※※※※

Love is intrinsically tragic. Who dares to love must be prepared to embrace the tragic for the sake of holding fast that which is loved.

The essence of the tragic is a collision between two or more values in real life where no single answer is the right one. The moral issues in life are layered and complex. Choices sometimes have to be made, and failure to act due to moral uncertainty may itself constitute betrayal of the human bond that unites us. The compassionate person is prepared to enter into the arena of the tragic for the sake of upholding human life in situations where the simple good is not possible. The moralist avoids the tragic by taking a stand for moral principle as having priority over real life choices.

※※※※※

The measure of strength as a virtue of character is not how much pressure one can exert against others but how much stress one can absorb without breaking apart. The strong person is not impervious to pain but persevering in purpose.

※※※※※

Serenity results from spiritual perception and spiritual counsel as the wisdom of God's Word and Spirit. Spiritual counsel gives vision, clarity, hope and healing to the self amidst conflict and confusion.

Serenity is not a feeling that comes by detaching oneself from inner conflicts and external threat. Nor is serenity achieved by seeking to escape from the ordinary into a state of extraordinary peace. Serenity is spiritual perception which integrates the extraordinary into the ordinary. When the vision of a larger purpose and meaning to life is brought into one's concrete situation and experience, a new picture comes into focus. Serenity is spiritual counsel which one receives into the soul as a deeper wisdom, such that a new capacity to grasp the whole of reality emerges. When spiritual perception and spiritual counsel do their work, spiritual healing results and the gift of serenity is received.

※※※※※

I live with the certainty of my own death. My death, I suppose, will be a loss for those who love me, and I can even speak of it as a loss of my own life. But it can never be a defeat. I am not in a "life-and-death" struggle, in which death can rob me of some hoped-for victory or prize.

❦❦❦❦

The love that God expresses can be tough as well as tender.

God's love has clear expectations which are realistic as well as purposeful. God's love is not a rushing torrent that devastates all in its path. Nor is God's love naive and idealistic, blind to the realities and complexities of life. Like God's love, human love is realistic and resourceful, but has its practical limits. One does not "simply" love and expect everything to work out. That is simplistic sentimentality.

Tough love is not brutal and unfeeling. It's toughness is not the absence of tenderness, but the practical realism of its expectations. Love has realistic expectations as to the yield on its investment. It also sets realistic criteria for measuring the goals it attempts to produce. The portfolio of love is set for high yield but low risk. The personal investment is total, but the expectations are in proportion to the growth potential.

❦❦❦❦

We should not be surprised by death, even when it comes when we don't expect it. As tragic as it may seem—and all deaths are a grievous loss—death is woven into the very fabric of life.

Holding my father's hands and feeling his last heart beat as his life slipped away, I realized that these were the hands that had held my newborn life and felt the pulse of my heart at birth. There is a time when hearts begin to beat, and there is a time when they stop. So begins and ends our allotted time on earth.

❦❦❦❦

Why is it that betrayal seems to be a failure that is so fatal?

I saw it printed in block letters with a blue felt tip pen across the top of the mirror in the men's restroom in a restaurant in San Francisco: **JUDAS COME HOME—ALL IS FORGIVEN!**

Could it be true? Would even Judas, the betrayer of Jesus, have found forgiveness if he had sought out the very one whom he had betrayed? Can God forgive anything and everything? Or does this bit of theological graffiti press beyond the limits of even divine love and grace?

We know that Judas was stricken with guilt and shame after having betrayed Jesus. Though he admitted his guilt and returned the money he had been paid to betray Jesus, he did not find forgiveness from others nor in himself. The darkness of despair closed in upon him—a night where there was no gentleness to provide healing and hope.

Judas reminds us that to love others and to make promises to others is to risk betrayal. Even as we point to the betrayal of others, we know that the seeds of betrayal lie hidden in our own best intentions.

Betrayal is felt to be an unforgivable act because it exposes ambivalence at the deepest core of human relationships. When we cannot trust our own trust, and dare not be loyal to loyalty, we feel the cords that bind together our deepest and most precious moments slip out of our grasp. Perhaps this is why, if a Devil did not exist, we would need to invent one. The defection of what once was good to become evil cries out for explanation. We can let neither God nor humankind bear the burden of introducing evil into what we all want to believe is essentially good.

Why is it that a single act of betrayal can destroy all of one's life? What is betrayal such a devastating failure that it has the power to condemn the past and contaminate the future? Why, for some, as in the case of Judas, does suicide appear to be the only personal atonement for betrayal?

The act of the betrayer not only contains the power to destroy a relationship, it tears at the very fabric of human society. The very concept of betrayal is grounded in a structure of community based on loyalty, trust and commitment. A lie is not betrayal until it destroys the bond of friendship. 'It is not the fact that you lied to me that is so terrible,' Nietszche once said, 'but the fact that I can no longer trust you.' Betrayal does more than deceive, it destroys trust in those who are deceived.

The other disciples certainly failed Jesus as well. Peter denied Jesus three times during the crucial hours of his trial. Without the resurrection of the crucified Jesus, there would have been no power of forgiveness in the cross. Without a deep personal encounter with the living Christ following the resurrection, the disciples would not have experienced forgiveness and healing of their shame.

But what of Judas? And what of each one of us who harbor secret shame and long for a reassuring word from Jesus?

Can we as children close doors that defy our attempts to open them as adults? I think so. I have them. I know they're there. Some of these doors are to keep me out rather than close me in. I no longer remember why they were closed, but only that they must be opened. Behind some doors lie undiscovered and unrevealed shame; behind others the bones of a child, who bears my name, buried in secret in order that the adult should live. These doors must opened and the child healed and led forth into life.

⁕⁕⁕⁕⁕⁕

As I grow toward health and wholeness, I believe that the resurrected Jesus will explore with me the still unopened doors and dispel unknown fears. He will give life to youthful dreams that perished in the anguish of failure, and release the child within to become the health of my older years. Not all doors can be opened at once. And so I live with rooms not yet invaded by his presence, for I also have spacious rooms that open outward toward the green prairies and undulating hills. And there are people in this landscape, moving toward me, and I am not afraid.

⁕⁕⁕⁕⁕⁕

A prayer for the dark night of the soul:

Reach out to me, Creator God, for what is to me an unbridgeable chasm is but the span of your hand extended in mercy. Shade your glory so that it may cast moonbeams across my night, for I am blinded by darkness. Come beside me, Lord Jesus, and bathe my face and anoint it with oil so that my countenance may shine with an inner peace and radiance that comes from peace. Flood my soul, Holy Spirit, with an unquenchable fountain of healing love.

Remember my forgetfulness, and rekindle in me the joy of being a child of God. Heal my memory of all self incrimination for past failures. Give me permission to be angry when I have been betrayed and to grieve when I have suffered loss. Listen to me when I pour out my complaints and don't stop me until I am finished, and then ask, 'Is there more?' Let me get to the bottom of all sadness and the end of all bitterness. Enable me to relinquish all regrets, free all the emotional prisoners I have taken, and awaken as from a deep sleep with the fever gone and a ravenous hunger for life restored. I love you Lord, and I lift my voice to worship you. Oh my soul rejoice. Take joy my King, in what you hear. Let me be a sweet, sweet sound in your ear. Amen.

References

Note: Sources are listed in each chapter in order of use, not in alphabetical order.

The quotation from Dag Hammarskjold is from <u>Markings</u>, New York: Knopf, 1966 p. 110.

Preface

The book by Michael Baker is <u>Dances with Wolves</u>, New York: Fawcett Gold Medal, 1988.

The reference to Samuel Augustus Maverick is from Clifford L. Egan, "Maverick, Samuel Augustus," <u>World Book Online Americas Edition</u>, http://ww.aolsvc.worldbook.aol.com/wbol/wbPage/na/ar/co/349780, April 28, 2001.

The reference to David Hubbard is from <u>Inarnational Ministry: The Presence of Christ in Church, Society and Family</u>, Essays in Honor of Ray S. Anderson, Christian D. Kettler, Todd H. Speidell, editors. Helmers and Howard Publishers, 1990. p. xi.

One. Introduction: The Making of a Maverick

I have drawn some of the material about my father from the book about my father, <u>Unspoken Wisdom: Truths My Father Taught Me</u> (Minneapolis: Augsburg Fortress, 1995).

The quotation from Christopher Fry is taken from *Three Plays*, "A Sleep of Prisoners" (New York, Oxford University Press, 1961), p. 209.

The comment about footnotes was made by Francisco Ayala, Professor of Biological Sciences at the University of

California, Irvine. The book which resulted was , <u>Whatever Happened to the Soul? Scientific and Theological Portraits of Human Nature</u>. Edited by Warren S. Brown, Nancy Murphy and H. Newton Malony, Fortress Press, 1998)—footnotes and all!

> Tell all the truth, but tell it slant—
> Success in Circuit lies
> Too bright for our infirm Delight!
> The Truth's superb surprise
> As Lightening to the Children eased
> With explanation kind
> The Truth must dazzle gradually
> Or every man be blind—
> > Emily Dickinson, <u>The Complete Poetry of Emily Dickinson</u>, Boston: Little Brown and Company, 1989

Two: Is Jesus an Evangelical?

The reference to Karl Barth is from <u>Church Dogmatics,</u> II/1, p. 55

The reference to Hans Küng is from, <u>Truthfulness: The Future of the Church</u>, London: Sheed and Ward, 1968.

Three: Does Jesus Think About Things Today?

The reference to the theologian who held that The Apostle Paul was wrong is Paul K. Jewett, in his book: <u>Man as Male and Female</u>. Grand Rapids: Eerdmans Publishing Company, 1975.

For a discussion of the resurrection of Jesus as hermeneutical criterion see my essay, "The Resurrection of Jesus as Hermeneutical Criterion," in <u>The Shape of Practical Theology: Empowering Ministry with Theological Praxis</u>. Downers Grove: InterVarsity Press, 2001, pp. 77-101.

The reference to Anthony Thistelton is: <u>New Horizons in Hermeneutics</u>. Glasgow: Harper Collins, 1992.

For a further discussion of the concept of a biblical antecedent and eschatological preference, see my book, The Soul of Ministry. Louisville: Westminster John Knox press, 1997, Chapter 14.

Four: Will Judas Be in Heaven?

The reference to my book on Judas is, The Gospel According to Judas: Is There a Limit to God's Forgiveness? Colorado Springs: NavPress, 1991

The references to Jacobus Arminius can be found in Arminius, Writings, 3 volumes, translation by James Nichols. Grand Rapids: Baker Book House, 1956, I:221ff.

For Barth's doctrine of election, see Church Dogmatics, II/1 pp. 3-194. On his concept of double predestination as completed solely in Jesus Christ see, pp. 162-167; for Barth's doctrine of justification and sanctification as completed in Jesus Christ for all persons, *de jure*, but not completed in fact (*de facto*) for all persons, see Church Dogmatics IV/1, pp. 145-148; IV/2, pp. 511ff.

The quotation by Donald Bloesch is from, Donald Bloesch, Theological Notebook: Volume II, 1964-1968. Colorado Springs: Helmers and Howard, 1991, pp. 82; 148

Five: What Do I Say At the Graveside of a Suicide?

The source from which I have drawn some facts about suicide as a crime is: The Facts of Death, by Michael Simpson, Englewood Cliffs, NH: Prentice-Hall, 1979.

The citation from Dietrich Bonhoeffer is from: Ethics, New York: Macmillan, 1955, p. 169.

The citation from Ernest Becker is in his book, The Denial of Death, New York: Free Press Paperbacks, Simon and Schuster, 1973, p. 145.

Six: Did Jesus Have to Do on a Cross?

Material in the introduction to this chapter has been drawn

from my book, The Soul of Ministry: Forming Leaders for God's People, Louisville: Westminster John Knox Press, 1977, Chapter Twelve.

The citation from Anselm is found in: Cur Deus Homo? LaSelle, Ill: Open Court Publishing Company, 1958, pp. 202; 246.

The citation from Calvin is found in: Institutes, Book II, chap. xvii, par. 4.

The citation from Abelard is found in: Dallas M. Roark, The Christian Faith, Nashville, Broadman Press, 1969. pp. 151-2.

The citation from Socinus is found in: Roark, The Christian Faith, pp. 155-6.

The citation from Otto Weber is found in: Foundations of Dogmatics. Grand Rapids: Eerdmans Publishing Co., 1983, Vol. 2, p. 213.

The citation from H. D. McDonald is found in: The Atonement of the Death of Christ. Grand Rapids: Baker, 1985, pp. 169, 172.

The citation from C. Norman Kraus is found in: Jesus Christ our Lord: Christology from a Disciple's Perspective. Scottdale, PA: 1987, p. 207.

The reference to Dietrich Bonhoeffer is from: Life Together, London: SCM Press, 1970, pp. 115-116.

The reference to Thomas F. Torrance is from: The Mediation of Christ. Colorado Springs: Helmers and Howard Publishers, 1992, pp. 110ff.

Seven: Do I have to Believe in Hell?

Portions of this chapter have been drawn from my book, Theology, Death and Dying, Basil Blackwell, 1986, Chapter Four. "Punishment after Death?"

The reference to Ibsen is cited by Merold Westphal, God, Guilt, and Death. Bloomington, IN: Indiana University Press, 1984, p. 119.

References to literature documenting concepts of punishment after death can be found in <u>The Judgment of the Dead: The Idea of Life after Death in the Major Religions</u>, by S. G. F. Brandon. New York: Charles Scribner, 1967.

The citation from Thomas Torrance is from: <u>Space, Time and Resurrection</u>. Grand Rapids: Eerdmans Publishing Company, 1976, p. 102. See also, Helmut Thielicke, <u>Being Human... Becoming Human</u>. Garden City, NY: Doubleday, 1984, pp. 116ff.

For the concept of the distinction between eternal punishing and eternal punishment I have drawn on the careful exegetical work of Samuel Bacchiocchi in <u>Immortality or Resurrection? A Biblical Study on Human Nature and Destiny</u>. Berrien Springs, MI: Biblical Perspectives, 1997, p. 207

The citation from Thomas Torrance with respect to "Questioning in Christ," is from <u>Theology in Reconstruction</u>. Grand Rapids: Eerdmans Publishing Company, 1965, p. 118.

The citation from Karl Barth is found in: Karl Barth, <u>Church Dogmatics</u>. III/3, p. 521. For Barth's treatment of hell and eternal torment, see <u>Church Dogmatics</u>, III/2, p. 603. See also <u>Church Dogmatics</u>, II/2, p. 496 for Barth's depiction of Jesus as the one "handed over" to hell on behalf of all so that no other need be.

Eight: Should I Pray for a Miracle?

The "faith formula" concept is discussed by Ken Blue in his book, <u>Authority to Heal</u>. InterVarsity Press, 1987, Chapter Three.

The references to John Baker are from, <u>Salvation and Wholeness</u>, London: Fountain Trust, 1973, pp. 21, 33-33.

The reference to T. J. McCrosson is from, <u>Bodily Healing and the Atonement</u>, by Dr. T. J. McCrossan; Edited by Roy Hicks and Kenneth E. Hagin. Faith Library Publications, n.d.

The reference to Gordon Fee is from his book, Gordon D. Fee, <u>The Disease of the Health and Wealth Gospels</u>. Costa Mesa, CA: The Word for Today, P.O. Box 800, 1979.

The reference to Colin Brown is from his book, <u>That You</u>

May Believe, Grand Rapids: Eerdmans Publishing Company, 1985, pp. 202f.

Nine: Goes God Allow Suffering to Produce Good?

In writing this chapter I have drawn on my book, Self Care: A Theology of Personal Empowerment and Spiritual Healing. Wheaton: Victor Books, 1995, Chapter Nine, pp. 184-203.

The reference from Harold Kushner can be found in his book, When Bad Things Happen to Good People. New York: Avon Books, 1981, p. 134.

The citation from Fyodor Dostoyevsky can be found in The Brothers Karamazov. New York: Random House, 1950), pp. 290-291.

The quotation by John Cobb and David Griffen is from the Los Angeles Times, Nov. 6, 1982, part II, p. 2.

Among some proponents of "open theism," are Clark Pinnock, Richard Rice, John Sanders, William Hasker, and David Basinger. See their book, The Openness of God: A Biblical Challenge to the Traditional Understand of God. Downers Grove: InterVarsity Press, 1994.

Ten: When Does Human Life Begin, And End?

The citation from Annie Dillard is from her book, An American Childhood. New York: Harper and Row, 1987, p. 11.

The reference to Karl Barth is from Church Dogmatics, III/1, chapter 28.

The reference to John Stoneking is from, "Saying Hello and Goodbye—Would I Baptize a Stillborn Baby?" The Circuit Rider, March, 1984, p. 3.

The incident regarding the woman who had the therapeutic abortion was taken from my book, On Being Human: Essays in Theological Anthropology. Grand Rapids: Eerdmans Publishing Company, 1982, p. 147.

The citations from Edward John Carnell are from his book, The Kingdom of Love and the Pride of Life. Grand Rapids: Eerdmans Publishing Company, 1960, pp. 16-17.

Eleven: Musings of a Maverick Theologian

The reference to G. J. Hamann is from: "J. G. Hamann and the Princess Gallitrzi," Philomathes, Robert Palmer and Robert Hamerton-Kelley (eds). The Hague: Martinus Nijhoff, p. 339.

The reference to telling the truth in Dietrich Bonhoeffer is from: Ethics. New York: Macmillan, 1955, pp. 64-65.

The reference to Heidegger is from: On the Way to Language, Martin Heidegger. New York: Harper and Row, p. 124.

The reference to Michael Polanyi is from: Personal Knowledge. London: Routledge and Kegan Paul, 1958, p. 322.

The quotation from Dietrich Bonhoeffer is from, Dietrich Bonhoeffer Works (German Edition), 13:360f. Cited by Andreas Pangritz, Karl Barth in the Theology of Dietrich Bonhoeffer, Eerdmans, 2000, p. 103.

The reference to Giordano Bruno in Dietrich Bonhoeffer is from: Letters and Papers From Prison. New York: Macmillan, 1971, p. 375.